Perfectionism and Contemporary Feminist Values

KIMBERLY A. YURACKO

Perfectionism and Contemporary Feminist Values

INDIANA
University Press

Bloomington & Indianapolis

50034999

11-3-03

This book is a publication of

Indiana University Press
601 North Morton Street
Bloomington, Indiana 47404-3797 USA

http://iupress.indiana.edu

Telephone orders 800-842-6796
Fax orders 812-855-7931
Orders by e-mail iuporder@indiana.edu

Manufactured in the United States of America

Library of Congress Cataloging-in-Publication Data

Yuracko, Kimberly A., date
    Perfectionism and contemporary feminist values / Kimberly A. Yuracko.
        p.   cm.
Includes bibliographical references and index.
    ISBN 0-253-34208-2 (hb : acid-free) — ISBN 0-253-21580-3 (pk : acid-free)
    1. Feminism. 2. Women—Psychology. I. Title.
    HQ1206 .Y87 2003
    305.42—dc21
                                                              2002009619

1 2 3 4 5   08 07 06 05 04 03

For Michael

Contents

Acknowledgments

This book has been a long time in the making, and it has benefited greatly from many people's help along the way. I am sure that neither Professor Susan Moller Okin nor Professor Mark Kelman had any idea of the magnitude or duration of the advising roles they were taking on when they began working with me while I was still in college. Susan Okin has both challenged and encouraged me on this project from its early stages as a Ph.D. dissertation to its present incarnation. Mark Kelman has read more drafts of this work than I wish to remind him of and was crucial in helping me structure (and restructure) the work as it evolved over the years. I am grateful to both of them for their longstanding mentoring and friendship.

Professors Debra Satz, Luis Fraga, and Margaret Jane Radin all helped me considerably in formulating the core ideas of the book. Professors Alan Wertheimer, Andrew Koppelman, Sherry Colb and several anonymous reviewers provided me with extremely helpful comments that motivated significant revisions and improvements to the project at very different stages. The Stanford Humanities Center, where I was a pre-doctoral fellow in 1995–96, provided me with the time, space, nutrition, and intellectual stimulation I needed to write the first draft of this book.

This project has also benefited greatly from the insights and encouragement of several friends and family members. I would like to thank Jennifer DiToro for engaging in many thoughtful conversations about the project and Jennifer Cuneo for reading and carefully commenting on several drafts. Cara Robertson has also read and provided careful criticisms of multiple drafts of this book. I am grateful for her insights and also for her unflagging encouragement, optimism, and good humor. I would like to thank my mother, Ellen Yuracko, for being my first role model; my father, William Yuracko, for being my first editor, and my sisters Kris Anderson and Kathy Yuracko for demonstrating vividly the diversity of roles encompassed within a good life. I would also like to thank my nephew Brennan Anderson for sharing in my excitement about this book and my niece Shelby Anderson for sharing with me her excitement about the world.

Several people have been instrumental in the final transformation of this manuscript into a book. I would like to thank Sara Kennedy for her excellent research assistance at the tail end of this project. I would also like to thank

Susanna Sturgis for her careful copyediting of the book and Marilyn Grob-schmidt and Jane Lyle of Indiana University Press for giving the manuscript a public life.

Finally, I would like to thank Michael Barsa for engaging in many hours of discussion about every part of this book and for his deft and patient editing of each chapter. I am deeply grateful to Michael for making, through his presence, both this project, and my life, immeasurably better than they would otherwise be.

Perfectionism and Contemporary Feminist Values

1   Introduction

Formal barriers to women's social and political participation have crumbled, yet society remains, to a significant degree, gendered in the roles that women and men play. Women's and men's choices regarding work and family are largely responsible for maintaining and reinforcing the differences. Women continue to have less social, economic, and political power than do men, and these differences are the apparent impetus for feminists' criticism of certain choices women make.

Many feminists recognize the importance of focusing on and challenging women's choices in order to change the status quo. However, most feminists hesitate to criticize women's choices directly or to blame women for playing a role in their social disempowerment. Feminists who fought to get women more options and control over their lives are reluctant to tell women they are making the wrong choices and directing their lives poorly. Therefore, instead of telling women they are making substantively bad choices, feminists most often challenge women's choices by pointing out perceived procedural flaws in the conditions under which the choices were made.

Feminists criticize women's choices most often by arguing that the choices were made under conditions that were illegitimately constrained. Ostensibly at least, feminists argue on behalf of seemingly neutral principles like liberty and equality and remain agnostic about how women should live their lives.[1] For example, instead of criticizing women's choices directly as incompatible with a meaningful life, feminists focus on the conditions under which women make their choices and argue that the conditions are neither sufficiently free nor equal to render the choices worthy of social respect. By advancing less controversial procedural and neutral-sounding arguments, feminists mask their real concerns about the substance of women's choices, relegating such concerns to something of a hidden agenda.

This book seeks to expose the hidden agenda of contemporary feminists, not in an attempt to argue that their conception of human flourishing is a dangerous or sinister one, but in an attempt to argue precisely the opposite. Encouraging women to live in accordance with a grounded and well-defined conception of human flourishing—what I call "perfectionism"—is the most effective way to redress the gender inequalities that stubbornly persist in our society. To this end, I not only seek to expose the perfectionist principles that undergird feminist writings, I also seek to articulate a concrete set of perfectionist principles that would improve the quality of individual women's lives and improve the social standing of women as a whole. I hope these principles can serve as a starting point for a more honest assessment of women's choices and the ramifications thereof.

By the early twenty-first century, American women had had access for several decades to virtually the same professions as men. Women are admitted on the same terms as men to vocational and professional training programs, and employers are legally prohibited from refusing to hire or promote women on the basis of gender. Yet, despite the seeming parity of such public-sphere opportunities, there remains a substantial difference in the degree, type, and remuneration of women's and men's participation in the labor force. Women spend fewer hours per week in paid employment than do men, they work in occupations that remain, to a considerable degree, segregated by sex, and they earn a fraction of what men do.[2]

Certainly some of the differences in women's and men's labor-force participation are due to old-fashioned employer discrimination. Undoubtedly, some employers do refuse to hire women for certain jobs, pay women less than men for the same job, and condone the sexual harassment and intimidation of female employees.[3] But employer discrimination does not explain all of the differences in kind and degree of women's and men's participation in the labor force. Discrimination is not the only reason that women have failed both to achieve economic parity with men and to fully integrate the workforce. At least some of the differences between women's and men's levels of labor-market participation result from different choices women and men make about how to structure and prioritize their lives.[4]

Even before entering the paid labor market, women and men make choices about what skills to develop and how much time and effort to invest in their future careers. To some degree, women and men continue to segregate themselves into different career paths, and many occupations remain highly sex-segregated. For example, although women earned approximately 56 percent of the bachelor's degrees awarded in 1997, they received 88 percent of the degrees awarded in home economics, 88 percent of the degrees awarded in library sciences, 82 percent of the degrees awarded in health sciences, and 75 percent of the degrees awarded in education. In contrast, men received 83.4 percent of the degrees awarded in engineering and 73 percent of the degrees awarded in computer and information sciences.[5]

Young women tend to invest less in their future market power because they, more so than young men, expect to become primary parents. Economist Victor Fuchs explains that "because most young women expect to be mothers, they (and their parents) are less likely than men to invest in wage-enhancing human capital while in school and in their first job or two after school."[6] In surveys of his undergraduate students at Stanford University, Fuchs found that although both male and female students valued marriage and career, when asked what changes they would make in their paid employment if they had young children, more than 60 percent of the women but fewer than 10 percent of the men said they would substantially reduce or stop altogether their paid employment.[7]

The different choices women and men make with respect to their educational investments translate into different career priorities and, not surprisingly, into different careers. Women choose to spend less time in the paid labor force than do men, both in terms of hours per week and years per lifetime. According to the 1994 Current Population Survey, 67 percent of single women as opposed to 74 percent of single men, and 61 percent of married women as opposed to 77 percent of married men were in the labor force.[8] Furthermore, approximately 67 percent of men between the ages of twenty and sixty-four work thirty-five hours or more per week as compared with 49 percent of women in the same age cohort.[9] Perhaps even more telling is that almost twice as many women as men were not in the labor force in 1994, and among those who said they were not currently looking for work, six times more women than men cited family responsibilities as the reason.[10] Not surprisingly, women spend fewer years of their lives in paid employment than do men[11] and have higher labor-force turnover rates.[12]

A 1992 survey of the Stanford Graduate School of Business class of 1982 graduates replicates the marked difference present nationally in women's and men's career paths. In 1992, 47 percent of the women graduates of 1982 worked full-time as compared with 82 percent of the men. Twenty-two percent of the women were self-employed as compared with 16 percent of the men. The big difference in work patterns came, however, in the numbers of women and men who worked part-time or were not employed outside the home. Twelve percent of the women as opposed to 1 percent of the men were employed part-time, and 19 percent of the women as opposed to 1 percent of the men were not employed ten years after graduation. The privileged position that these women hold in the job market and the fact that 64 percent of them, as compared to 26 percent of the men, said that they have made a career change for lifestyle reasons, suggests that different life choices play a major role in the different career paths of these women and men.

Women and men also value aspects of their work differently, and their career choices reflect attempts to maximize their most desired job characteristics. Writes economist Randall Filer, "Men and women systematically report that, on average, they value particular features of their jobs differently. For example, men tend to attach more importance to pecuniary rewards (wages and fringe benefits) while women value interpersonal and other non wage aspects of the job more highly."[13] Women look for and find jobs that require less commuting time and allow for more flexibility with respect to time off than do jobs typically held by men.[14]

Again, these general predictions hold true for the narrower set of Stanford Business School graduates as well. Thirty-three percent of the women graduates of 1982 who worked full-time reported spending no nights away from home each month on business, compared to 8 percent of the men. Moreover, only 24 percent of the women who worked full-time spent five days or more a month away from home, compared to 42 percent of the men.[15]

Not surprisingly, these choices help maintain a heavily sex-segregated labor force. Women make up over 90 percent of all nursery school and kindergarten teachers, secretaries, and registered nurses, as well as over 85 percent of all elementary school teachers.[16] Men make up over 90 percent of automobile mechanics, construction workers, truck drivers, and engineers, as well as over 75 percent of physicians and lawyers.[17]

In light of the data indicating a persistent difference in men's and women's public-sphere participation, this book focuses on three choices that are distinctly gendered and frequently criticized by feminists. These are women's choices to commodify their sexuality, to objectify their sexuality, and to become full-time homemakers. As will be discussed in more detail later, women commodify their sexuality when they exchange access to some form of their sexuality for money or other goods. Women objectify their sexuality when they conceive of their sexual and physical selves as deriving their value from and existing for men. I assess a range of feminists' arguments criticizing these choices. These choices are important in reinforcing the divergent life patterns of women and men, yet they are difficult for feminists to criticize by resorting only to neutral principles.

To make their criticisms most acceptable and least offensive to a liberal society, feminists couch their arguments in terms of generally accepted and seemingly neutral principles of liberty and equality. Liberalism is a theory based on individual rights and social agnosticism toward what people do with these rights. Liberal theories are rights-based and value-neutral. Accordingly, feminists try to avoid the appearance of making value-laden judgments about how women should and should not live their lives. Feminists try to avoid appearing to criticize choices because of what the choices substantively entail.

Despite feminists' attempts to frame their criticisms of certain choices as arguments on behalf of freedom or equality, these principles are inadequate to justify and explain feminists' objections.[18] These seemingly neutral principles are simply unable to explain or justify feminists' criticism of these choices.

In actuality, feminists' arguments are driven by perfectionism, not neutral principles. Perfectionism is the endorsement of a vision of human flourishing and the recognition that certain ways of life are compatible with this vision while others are not. Perfectionist theories are value-based conceptions of the good life. Conceptions of human flourishing better explain and justify feminists' opposition to the choices described than do the liberal rationales most frequently asserted.

While liberalism and perfectionism are not as starkly opposed as I have suggested, the arguments I call perfectionist in this book do not fall near the fuzzy line separating the two. Liberalism does endorse values such as autonomy, bodily integrity, and self-respect that are at root probably most strongly grounded in a vision of human flourishing.[19] According to William Galston, "every contemporary liberal theory relies, explicitly or tacitly, on the same triadic theory of the good, which asserts the worth of human existence, the value of the fulfillment of human purposes, and the commitment to rationality as the chief guide to both individual purposiveness and collective undertakings."[20]

The arguments I describe as perfectionist endorse a far more substantial and controversial conception of human flourishing. They cannot be confused with the values commonly endorsed by liberals. For example, the arguments that I describe as perfectionist endorse not simply autonomy but autonomy directed toward intellectual and rational development, not simply self-respect but self-respect grounded in one's worth as a social and intellectual actor. The perfectionist values I describe and endorse are more substantive and specific than the values commonly accepted as liberal rights.

Perfectionism, however, need not require the social endorsement of a single way of life. A pluralistic perfectionism allows for a wide range of acceptable life patterns, projects, and beliefs, all of which are compatible with human flourishing. A theory is perfectionist simply because some life projects are not part of the acceptable range.

The problem with perfectionism is that it frightens people. There is a fear that the moral aspects of a perfectionist theory will automatically and neces-sarily lead to coercive and totalitarian political theories. Sometimes it seems people feel perfectionist moral theorizing itself is not worth the political risks. This quick association of perfectionist moral theory with coercive po-litical theory is a mistake.

Perfectionist moral theories alone, even without accompanying political theories, are powerful tools for challenging individuals' choices and changing the way people live their lives. It is vitally important for each individual pri-vately to think about and determine for herself what constitutes a meaningful life even if society as a whole is not structured to promote this vision. There is a private realm of behavior in which individuals form their own priorities, make decisions about their own lives, and influence the decisions of those around them, not through coercion but through social approval or friendly argument. This is the realm in which attitudes and behaviors are formed. It is also the realm in which perfectionist theories can and do have the most impact on people's lives even absent any political theory of social coercion. People's reluctance in our society to criticize other individuals' life choices goes beyond an unwillingness to support state intervention with respect to a particular choice. Developing a theoretical basis to criticize one's own choices and those of others is itself an important contribution of perfectionism.

Additionally, the split between a privately focused moral theory and a pub-licly focused political theory is not as great as it may first seem. It is a mistake to associate political theory with only the most coercive possible aspects of a social structure. There is a complex web of social subsidies and social margi-nalization for different attitudes and behaviors that looks more political than personal and yet does not rise to the level of social coercion. Consider the social institution of public education. The mission of schools is to educate and inculcate children with social values. Schools cannot help but socialize children. They do this generally not by coercing children to make certain choices but through a process of encouragement, discouragement, and mar-ginalization of different choices. For example, high school guidance counsel-ors do not present to graduating girls the options of exotic dancer or porno-graphic model as choices to be compared in terms of their pros and cons against other choices, such as doctor or construction worker. The choices of exotic dancer or pornographic model are both discouraged and culturally marginalized. They are not presented neutrally as two options to be weighed against others. In this way, perfectionist judgments already influence and di-rect individual behavior without taking the form of coercive state action. My goal is to bring out into the open the perfectionist beliefs that permeate femi-nists' writings and show why an open endorsement of perfectionism is necessary to both improve the quality of women's lives and to encourage a more substantive equality between the sexes.

This book is organized into three parts. Part I sets up the two distinct problems that engage this book: first, the phenomenon of women's seemingly bad choices and the narrow range of arguments feminists use to criticize these choices; second, the theoretical inadequacy of contemporary perfectionism to provide an alternative explanation for feminists' criticisms.

Through the placement of theoretical perfectionism next to a discussion of practical feminism, part I raises the fundamental questions of the book. Does it make sense to criticize women's choices without reference to a theory of perfectionism? If not, what is the best perfectionist theory on which to ground the criticisms?

Part II answers the first question by pointing out the limits of feminists' ability to criticize women's choices by relying on and promoting neutral principles. In these chapters, I analyze various freedom- and equality-based arguments commonly put forth by feminists for criticizing and challenging the validity of women's choices. Feminists argue that women's choices are the product of coercion, sexist socialization, and choice sets that are inferior to men's. Feminists also argue women's choices will make them vulnerable to future harms. I show that feminists' truly neutral and nonperfectionist arguments can justify only a small subset of their choice critiques. In order to criticize the full range of choices they want to criticize, feminists rely covertly on underlying perfectionist principles.

Finally, part III attempts to develop a pragmatic perfectionism that will avoid the problems of contemporary perfectionist theories while providing a stronger and more accurate basis for challenging the choices so many feminists find objectionable. The useful work of perfectionism, and the work that has yet to be done sufficiently, is in grounding perfectionism in real-world situations and experiences. Instead of starting from a single abstract premise, I begin with four narrowly drawn perfectionist principles. These perfectionist principles better explain and justify feminist opposition to the range of choices discussed than do the nonperfectionist arguments that are more commonly relied upon. Furthermore, they offer a springboard for the broader feminist challenge to choices and situations that cannot be adequately challenged and criticized within a liberal rubric.

PART ONE. FEMINISM AND PERFECTIONISM

Two problems set the stage for this book. The first is the problem of women's seemingly bad life choices. The second is the inadequacy of existing perfectionist theories to explain why these choices are bad. It is the collision of these problems that forms the basis for the rest of the book.

Most feminists avoid criticizing choices directly by focusing instead on the conditions under which choices are made. They argue about whether women's choices are made under conditions which are sufficiently free and equal to permit the choices to be respected. They avoid appearing to criticize choices or activities directly as simply incompatible with a valuable human life. These arguments are, however, just beneath the surface.

Feminists' neutral-sounding arguments cannot in fact justify or explain their criticisms of the choices discussed in this book. A conception of human flourishing—that is, a vision of what a good life looks like—necessarily informs and directs their arguments.

Yet the perfectionism lurking in feminists' choice critiques is not reflective of or explained by current perfectionist theories. Feminists need a perfectionist theory that has not yet been articulated to explain what they find problematic about certain choices.

Chapter 2 has two purposes. First, it introduces feminists' debates about women's choices to become sex workers, sex kittens, and full-time housewives.[1] Second, it shows that feminists criticize these choices by relying, almost exclusively, on procedural and neutral-sounding arguments.

The purpose of chapter 3 is to introduce an alternative nonneutral justification for challenging women's choices. Perfectionism is the belief that there are better and worse ways to live a life and that certain values and activities are compatible with human flourishing while others are not. Perfectionist theories justify criticizing choices directly and substantively based on their compatibility with human flourishing. Chapter 3 describes the abstract perfectionisms of Joseph Raz, Thomas Hurka, and George Sher as well as the far more grounded perfectionism of Martha Nussbaum. The chapter argues that while these perfectionisms are useful for their own purposes of presenting perfectionism as a theoretically viable alternative to liberalism, both the abstract and grounded perfectionisms presented here are unable to offer any real guidance to citizens in western industrialized countries about how to live their lives.

2 Three Hard Choices

This book focuses on three types of choices that are problematic for feminist theorists and activists.[1] It focuses on women's choices to commodify their sexuality in the marketplace; to sexually objectify themselves for men, albeit without a direct exchange of sex for goods; and to leave the paid workforce in order to become full-time homemakers. I have chosen to focus on these three choices because they are troubling and divisive not only for feminists but for the public at large.

There are, of course, feminists who are not critical of these choices. Prostitution in particular has sparked sharp feminist debate with many feminists arguing that prostitution is a legitimate work option worthy of respect. Overall, however, these three choices have probably received more attention and criticism from feminists than any other choices women commonly make. This chapter analyzes the arguments offered by feminists both in support of and in opposition to these choices in order to show the narrow procedural form these arguments take. It reveals the most commonly used arguments for challenging the legitimacy and validity of these choices in order to make clear feminists' efforts to frame their criticisms of women's choices in neutral procedural terms and to avoid more threatening arguments based on the value and meaning of the choice itself.

Feminist choice critiques can be thought of along a continuum. At one end are those feminists who claim that women's choices to be sex workers, sex kittens, or full-time homemakers are sufficiently free to be worthy of social respect. At the other end are those feminists who claim that women's choices are coerced and constrained, rendering the choices socially illegitimate and unacceptable.[2] The debate is framed in terms of the conditions under which women should make their life choices in order for those choices to be deserving of social respect. The two sides disagree about both what constitutes sufficiently free and equal conditions and what constitutes the reality of women's experiences. However, by focusing on the conditions under which women make their choices, feminists on both ends of this continuum share the implicit assumption that choices made under sufficiently free and equal conditions are worthy of respect—regardless of the nature of the choice—while those that are not made under adequate conditions are not worthy of such respect. This chapter explores how this focus on procedures and conditions along with a professed neutrality to the substance of choices frames feminists' criticism of the three socially controversial choices at issue in this book. The next part of the book will assess the genuineness and effectiveness of these arguments.

I. Women as Sex Workers

The debate among feminists about whether society should legitimize women's sexual commodification has been a heated one for many years. The debate is loudest and most clearly defined with respect to women's choices to become prostitutes, as opposed to other forms of sexual commodification like lap dancing or stripping. For example, some feminists argue for the continued and intensified prohibition of prostitution while others argue for either decriminalization of prostitution—which would eliminate laws prohibiting prostitution and allow prostitutes to work without fear of state prosecution— or legalization—which is usually understood as leading to state regulation of prostitution.[3] At root, however, the debate over prostitution, as well as over other forms of sex work, is a debate over the kinds of conditions under which women must make their choices. In particular, feminists on both sides of the debate focus on whether choices are (1) freely made, and (2) made from an adequate range of options.

Feminists like Priscilla Alexander and Gail Pheterson, who support women's choice to commodify their sexuality, argue that the choices are usually freely made.[4] Their claim relies on a strict distinction between coerced and free choices and, correspondingly, between forced and voluntary prostitution.

According to the National Task Force on Prostitution, "Voluntary prostitution is the mutually voluntary exchange of sexual services for money or other consideration; it is a form of work. . . . Forced prostitution is a form of aggravated assault."[5] Pro-sex-work feminists believe and respect the sentiments of sex workers like Mary Johnson, a stripper, who argues that "we [strippers and prostitutes] have chosen our profession for whatever reasons. I may not have decided when I was five years old that when I grew up, I wanted to be a stripper, but just the same, I did make a choice at one point."[6] For pro-sex-work feminists, coerced choices are only those made in response to actual threats of violence. The woman who hands over her wallet to the mugger who points a gun at her is coerced, as is the woman who engages in sex under the same circumstances. Women who engage in sex for money because they are poor, do not have other job opportunities, and do not have other skills are not coerced under this standard liberal model.[7]

Priscilla Alexander, for example, argues that only prostitution resulting from traditional forms of coercion is problematic. She believes that "[t]he issue of forced prostitution is often used to obscure the issue of the right of women to work as prostitutes."[8] Alexander estimates that in the United States only about 10 percent of prostitutes are coerced into it by third parties through a "combination of trickery and violence."[9] Presumably, the other 90 percent have chosen to commodify their sexuality in a manner that is sufficiently uncoerced to satisfy Alexander.

Feminists who respect women's choices to sell their sexuality do acknowledge that some women are forced into prostitution but argue that simply because some women are coerced does not mean that all women are. Moreover, such feminists argue that we should not expand our conception of coercion to include the economic conditions under which women frequently choose to enter sex work. Doing so would not only deflate the meaning and importance of coercion but would lead to a challenge of virtually all the decisions poor people make about how to structure their lives. The choice to become a sex worker does not look any less free than many other economically constrained choices people make about how to live their lives—like going to a public rather than private university or becoming a secretary rather than an artist. Challenging all such choices would be a pointless and patronizing attack on self-determination, such feminists argue.

Alexander, for example, argues that while most women who enter the sex industry do so because they need money, this does not undermine the authenticity of the choice. "In any society, people make decisions about work based on some kind of evaluation of the options open to them."[10]

In more graphic terms, Peggy Morgan, an erotic dancer in Boston, affirms that the nature of the work or the economic conditions under which it is chosen should not be used to challenge the rationality or integrity of the choice to become a sex worker. Morgan argues that "[n]obody enjoys being pawed, poked, prodded, and fucked by men we wouldn't give the time of day if we met them elsewhere. . . . The fact is, there's a livable wage to be made in the sex business, and *we* decide when, where and with whom we'll do what."[11] For Morgan, because sex work may reflect a woman's autonomy and self-determination, it is worthy of social respect.

Some feminists argue that prostitution is not inherently different from other kinds of manual and physical work that people choose under economically constrained conditions.[12] This view is well reflected in a statement by English sex worker Eva Rosta. Rosta argues that "women and men and feminists have to realize that all work involves selling some part of your body. You might sell your brain, you might sell your back, you might sell your fingers for typewriting. Whatever it is that you do you are selling one part of your body. I choose to sell my body the way I want to and I choose to sell my vagina."[13] Peggy Morgan agrees. She explains that "[h]aving a customer fondle a breast, for instance, may not be pleasant, especially if he's rough, but it doesn't feel like being violated. It's part of a job, and really no different than if he touched an elbow. It's not sexual; it's *work*."[14]

Attestations of the "happy hooker" do exist and provide added leverage to arguments that prostitution is freely chosen. Peggy Miller, founder of the Canadian Organization for the Rights of Prostitutes, argues that she enjoys her work as a prostitute. Writes Miller, "'There are lots of whores out there who, despite the terrible legal and social environment, enjoy our work."[15] Although not directly proving that women freely choose to commodify their sexuality, statements from women who enjoy selling their sexuality reinforce arguments in favor of the legitimacy of the choices. The claim that some women enjoy the work suggests that it is certainly plausible that they have freely chosen it. Moreover, if sex workers enjoy their work, then they are probably not being harmed in ways that would require a liberal state to intervene on their behalf.

The arguments challenging the legitimacy and validity of women's choices to commodify their sexuality mirror those we have just seen in one crucial respect: the bulk of the arguments focus on the freedom of the decision maker. One major reason feminists offer for challenging women's choices is that the choices are the product of coercion. Feminists who oppose sex work, however, typically adopt broader conceptions of coercion than do feminists on the other side. Anti-sex-work feminists often consider coerced not only choices made in response to threats of physical violence, but also choices made in response to economic need, and even choices made in response to offers that are hard to resist.

The strongest, and most standard, coercion-based challenge to women's choices to commodify their sexuality argues that many, if not all, women who choose to commodify their sexuality do so in response to direct threats of physical violence. Just as a bank teller's choice to hand over money in response to a gun pointed at her head is considered invalid—not a real choice—so too is a woman's choice to sell her sexuality in response to threatened abuse.

Catharine MacKinnon is probably the best-known proponent of this viewpoint. MacKinnon argues that "most if not all prostitution is ringed with force in the most conventional sense, from incest to kidnapping to forced drugging to assault."[16] According to MacKinnon, violence is the norm by which women are forced into sex work and forced to remain sex workers.[17]

Margaret Baldwin agrees arguing that "prostitution is often compelled by physical force or its threat, by physical and mental torture, by kidnapping."[18]

The activist group WHISPER (Women Hurt in Systems of Prostitution Engaged in Revolt), devoted to helping women escape from prostitution, also takes this view. According to WHISPER, "Every time a prostitute climbs into a car or walks into a hotel with a strange man, coerced by the circumstances of her existence, sexual abuse, rape battery or just plain poverty, she risks her freedom and her very life. Can we then say that prostitution is a valid occupational alternative that she freely chooses?"[19] Susan Kay Hunter argues that "[p]rostitution is unwanted sex. It is sex that she says 'yes' to, but it is the kind of 'yes' that is uttered under circumstances devoid of choice. Most men do not know what it means to be this deprived: she is beaten, she is pimped, she is not free, she is not present in her own body."[20]

Feminists who object to sex work often also consider coerced choices that are made under conditions of economic necessity. WHISPER reflects this expanded version of coercion when it argues that "[p]rostitution is founded on enforced sexual abuse under a system of male supremacy that is itself built along a continuum of coercion—fear, force, racism and poverty."[21]

Claims of economic coercion come in stronger and weaker versions. The stronger version argues that women are forced to sell their sexuality because it is their only means for survival. WHISPER suggests this version of economic coercion when it claims that "many [prostitutes] were battered women who have escaped from, or were abandoned by, abusive husbands and forced into prostitution in order to support themselves and their children."[22] MacKinnon, too, argues that economic necessity forces women to commodify their sexuality, but she also recognizes that such economic necessity is not accepted as a standard form of coercion. MacKinnon explains that "[s]ex-based poverty, both prior to and during prostitution, enforces it; while poverty alone has not been recognized as making out a case of coercion, it has been recognized as making exit impossible in many cases in which coercion has been found."[23]

The weaker version of economic coercion argues that women are forced into sex work because the work provides their best, although not their only, means for survival. MacKinnon also challenges women's choices using this weaker version of economic coercion. MacKinnon argues that the "fact that prostitution and modeling are structurally women's best economic options should give pause to those who would consider women's presence there a true act of free choice."[24] This version of coercion is also reflected in Peggy Morgan's description of the exotic dancers she knew in the Combat Zone in Boston. According to Morgan:

Most dancers are straight, in their early twenties, and from poor or work-ing class backgrounds. Some graduated from working the streets, a few still work for pimps. Many are single mothers working to supplement their meager welfare checks. Beyond meeting the basic necessities for food, clothing and shelter, working in the Combat Zone is the only way they can afford the symbols of success that society has dangled in front of them all their lives: nice clothes, jewelry, cocaine, eating out in fine restaurants.[25]

Anti-sex-work feminists also challenge women's choices to commodify their sexuality on the grounds that the choices are made under conditions of and in response to pervasive sexist socialization. The socialization argument that is closest to a standard coercion argument claims that although women may not choose to commodify their sexuality in response to a particular threat to their health or safety, they make this choice in response to a more general pattern of sexual violence and abuse in their lives. While discrete acts of sexual commodification may not be performed in response to discrete threats, women's decisions to commodify and sell their sexuality are made in response to a larger pattern of sexual abuse over the course of the women's lives. For example, a particular woman who prostitutes herself on a given night may not be doing so because she is threatened with physical violence if she refuses. However, this same woman may have been beaten up on many prior occasions for trying to refuse sex to men so that she no longer thinks of attempting to refuse sex to the men who want it from her. The argument is that because women's choices to commodify their sexuality arise under conditions where they are taught through the prevalence of sexual violence that sex is really what they are for, their choices to commodify themselves are not sufficiently autonomous.[26]

MacKinnon suggests that the method by which women are socialized ren-ders all women's choices suspect, but she focuses particular attention on those choices that are related to sexuality. Women are socialized through systemic sexual violence to sexualize their own subordination. MacKinnon reminds us that "more than one-third of all girls experience sex, perhaps are sexually ini-tiated, under conditions that even this society recognizes are forced or at least unequal. Perhaps they learn this process of sexualized dominance as sex. Top-down relations feel sexual."[27] MacKinnon argues that the violent socialization that shapes women's sense of self and forms their preferences also diminishes the weight to be given to their choices to commodify their sexuality. Accord-ing to MacKinnon, "The fact that most women in prostitution were sexually abused as children, and most entered prostitution itself before they were adults, undermines the patina of freedom and the glamour of liberation" that the sex industry tries to convey about its participants.[28] For MacKinnon, the choices are not free enough.

The more general socialization argument is that even if individual women are not the direct victims of prior sexual abuse, all women are taught through pornography, advertising, and the prevalence of sexual violence against women that women are to be valued and used sexually. The idea is that women's choices are the product of sexist socialization and women would not make them under conditions of gender equality. Again, women's choices do not appear to be free enough.

According to WHISPER, "Prostitution is taught in the home, socially validated by a sexual libertarian ideology, and enforced by both the church and the state."[29] Because all women are indoctrinated with strong messages about their purpose in society as being for sex, women's decision to commodify their sexuality cannot then be accepted unquestioningly as authentic and freely made. MacKinnon makes the same argument:

> If women are socially defined such that female sexuality cannot be lived or spoken or felt or even somatically sensed apart from its enforced definition, so that it *is* its own lack, then there is no such thing as a woman as such, there are only walking embodiments of men's projected needs. For feminism, asking whether there is, socially, a female sexuality is the same as asking whether women exist.[30]

Similarly, anti-sex-work feminists challenge women's choices on the grounds that under conditions of inequality women's life options are different from, and perhaps more constrained than, men's. In light of their options, women's choices to become sex workers do not seem sufficiently free. MacKinnon, for example, argues that "[w]omen's precluded options in societies that discriminate on the basis of sex, including in employment, are fundamental to the prostitution context. If prostitution is a free choice, why are the women with the fewest choices the ones most often found doing it."[31]

WHISPER, too, rejects "the lie that women freely choose prostitution from a whole array of economic alternatives that exist under civil equity."[32] According to WHISPER:

> Eighty percent of the people in poverty in this country are women with dependent children. Women earn approximately sixty-seven cents for every dollar men earn. It is estimated that one out of every four girls will be sexually abused before the age of sixteen, that a woman is battered every eighteen seconds, raped every four minutes, that two thousand to four thousand women are beaten to death by their husbands annually . . . [33]

Under social conditions in which women's options look dramatically different and, according to WHISPER, dramatically worse than men's, women's choices to commodify their sexuality cannot be assumed to reflect an act of real agency.

Susan Kay Hunter agrees. Because women's life choices are constrained, their choices to commodify their sexuality cannot be accepted unquestioningly. Hunter asks us to "explore the meaning of 'choice' in prostitution by looking at the sphere of choices available to or withheld from all women. . . . Right now for all women choices are severely limited by the poor, second class status dealt to us."[34] Hunter argues that women's career and financial prospects are considerably worse than men's, leaving women dependent on men in order to avoid poverty.

A slightly different anti-sex-work argument is based on future vulnerability rather than on a present lack of options. The problem with the choice is not the conditions under which the choice was made but the conditions the choice will lead to. Under this line of argument, regardless of what initially motivates women to enter the industry, they will be subject to extremely high levels of physical and emotional violence once they do. The argument is not that the decision itself was not freely made, but that the decision will result in a loss of freedom in the future. In other words, this vulnerability argument challenges the legitimacy of the sex-worker choice because of the high risk of future rights violations that the choice entails.

MacKinnon argues that violence for women in prostitution is the norm: "It is common for prostitutes to be deprived of food and sleep and money, beaten, tortured, raped, and threatened with their lives, both as acts for which the pimp is paid by other men, and to keep the women in line. Women in prostitution are subject to near total domination."[35] Nancy Erbe agrees that once women enter prostitution they are subject to physical and emotional violence and are often unable to escape: "Regardless of how women are procured for prostitution, pimps control prostitutes after they enter prostitution."[36]

II. Sexual Objectification

The decision of women to conceive of themselves as sexual objects for male enjoyment has far fewer feminist defenders than does the decision of women to prostitute themselves. Again though, the arguments, both in favor of and in opposition to the choice, focus on the conditions under which choices are made. Unlike the narrow sex-for-money exchange involved in prostitution, sexual objectification refers to a broad array of activities and behavior that women undertake in order to maximize their value as sexual objects in the eyes of the men with whom they are interacting. Women may objectify themselves by wearing sexually suggestive clothing, by spending a great deal of time on their clothing or makeup, by adopting flirtatious or sexually suggestive mannerisms, or by becoming sexually available. Almost all women do one or more of these things at certain times. Indeed, the ubiquity of women's self-objectification is part of what makes the choice such a tricky one to challenge.

Generally, feminists' arguments supporting and criticizing women's choices to sexually objectify themselves parallel feminists' arguments made in response to women's choices to commodify their sexuality. The focus is on whether women's choices are sufficiently free.

Feminists who respect women's choices to maximize their object status for men and to gain whatever rewards are possible as a result of their object status argue that these choices are freely made. Women may freely and rationally choose to maximize their object status in order to reap the rewards from such a choice. According to these feminists, such a choice is as legitimate as a woman's choice to maximize her value as an intellectual being. Karen Lehrman, for example, argues in the *Lipstick Proviso* that "[s]ex can be a great and quick leveler for women; just as some will probably always sell their bodies for money, others will do so for power. We might not like this, and we might try to minimize the situations that lead women to think this is their only option, but women have as much of a right to do this as to, say, feed the homeless."[37] Lehrman argues that there is no conflict between a woman taking cosmetic or surgical steps to maximize her beauty and still being a feminist.[38] Lehrman stresses that a pursuit of beauty can be freely chosen and need not be "mindless."[39]

Much more feminist ink has been spent arguing that women's choices to become sexual objects are not sufficiently free.[40] Naomi Wolf argues, for example, that women may be denied the privileges of social membership if they refuse to participate in the universal ritual of female sexual objectification. According to Wolf, women are threatened with social ostracism if they refuse to sexually objectify themselves. Wolf argues that such threats, while not rising to the level of physical violence, are nonetheless significant and coercive. "Men," according to Wolf, "usually think of coercion as a threatened loss of autonomy—for women, coercion often takes a different form: the threat of losing the chance to form bonds with others, be loved, and stay wanted. Men think coercion happens mainly through physical violence, but women see physical suffering as bearable compared with the pain of losing love."[41]

Wolf also explains that "[w]omen learn what we have to do from our environment. Women are sensitive to the signals that institutions send about what we have to do with our 'beauty' to survive, and the institutions are giving us a very clear message that they endorse any level of violence."[42] Women suffer starvation and painful surgeries in order to avoid the threatened social invisibility that comes with women's refusal to become, or to continue to be, sex objects appealing to men.

In addition to claims of coercion, feminists also argue that women's choices to objectify their sexuality are the product of broader sexist socialization. Girls and women are socialized by pervasive sexual violence to conceptualize their self and social worth in terms of their status as sex objects.

MacKinnon argues that women come to understand who they are, what they are for, and for whom by being raised in a society characterized by systemic sexualized violence against women and saturated with pornography. Women internalize the lessons of sexual violence and the message of pornography and come to experience themselves as available sex objects.[43] Moreover, they experience their objecthood as sexual. MacKinnon describes the power of pornography to define women both for themselves and for men:

> I draw on pornography for its form and content, for the gaze that eroticizes the despised, the demeaned, the accessible, the there-to-be-used, the servile, the child-like, the passive, and the animal. *That* is the content of the sexuality that defines gender female in this culture, and visual thingification is its method.[44]

MacKinnon explains how systemic sexual violence against women in general leads women in particular—even those not directly the victims of violence—to make choices about their lives under conditions that are less than free. According to MacKinnon, women's socialization through pornography and sexual violence perversely distorts their preferences. MacKinnon explains:

> If the existing social model and reality of sexuality center on male force, and if that sex is socially learned and ideologically considered positive and is rewarded, what is surprising is that not all women eroticize dominance, not all love pornography, and many resent rape. . . . Given the statistical realities, much of women's sexual lives will occur under post-traumatic stress. Being surrounded by pornography—which is not only socially ubiquitous but often directly used as part of sex—makes this a relatively constant condition. Women cope with objectification through trying to meet the male standard, and measure their self-worth by the degree to which they succeed.[45]

A more general socialization-based choice critique claims that girls are encouraged to think of themselves as decorative objects for others' enjoyment and are rewarded socially for their self-objectification. Girls are praised and receive attention because of their physical attractiveness. These girls grow into women who know that their social value depends largely on their physical attractiveness. They are taught that their social value depends on their beauty quotient. Women choose to sexually objectify themselves and to maximize their sex-object value because they know that their highest, if not their only, social value comes from their sex-object status. Writes Rita Freedman: "While many idols are denied to females, that of beauty object is subtly as well as overtly encouraged. To enact femininity is to become a kind of exhibitionist, to display oneself as a decorative object."[46] "Women are taught the standards currently worshipped as ideal and taught to equate self-worth with appearance."[47]

Feminists also challenge women's choices to objectify themselves because of the likelihood that such choices will lead to the women's future vulnerability—that is, the choices will lead to women's future loss of freedom and future constrained choices. Women should be discouraged from choosing to objectify themselves because these choices involve high future costs that women are unlikely to adequately consider. As a result, women are likely to regret their decisions in the future.

Freedman suggests this vulnerability-based argument when she describes a forty-two-year-old woman who sexually objectified herself as a child and young woman. Because she was conventionally beautiful she received a great deal of social recognition and had high social value as a sex object. As she reached middle age and her value as an object began to diminish, the woman, whose worth to both society and herself was conceived of only in terms of her object status, suffered severe anxiety attacks and a loss of self-esteem. The woman who had relied exclusively on her value as a sex object for social acceptance, recognition, and accomplishment did not have other skills and virtues to rely on for her sense of self-worth. The self-objectified woman "failed to establish a broader base of self-esteem and failed to recognize or cultivate other strengths."[48]

III. Becoming a Full-Time Homemaker

The choice to become a full-time homemaker has also engendered almost uniform criticism from feminists. As with the other choices, both what support and what criticism exists for the choice among feminists is largely framed in terms of the adequacy or inadequacy of the conditions under which the choice was made.

Karen Lehrman, for example, argues the choice should be accepted uncritically as long as it is made under adequately free conditions. Lehrman sums up this position vividly when she claims that "under a liberal feminist society, all women could spend their days needle pointing 'Home Sweet Home' samplers—as long as their choices are being made 'freely.'"[49]

Whether the choice is freely made is, of course, a large part of the debate. Feminists who challenge women's choice to be full-time homemakers argue that women are "forced" into becoming full-time homemakers by social convention and community expectation. They question the validity of the choice using arguments that blur the distinction between coercion and socialization.

Feminists do not argue that women are, with any frequency, coerced by threats of violence to be full-time homemakers. Instead they argue that women are pressured into making such choices by social expectations and by the ideal of the stay-at-home mom. Reva Landau blurs the language of coercion and socialization in her challenge of this choice. Landau argues:

> As long as men who work outside the home are considered good fathers,
> while women who work outside the home are not considered to be good
> mothers, as long as it is considered to be the mother's duty, and not the
> father's duty, to take care of the children, to clean the house, to clean
> the clothes, to buy the clothes, to pick up the laundry, etc., etc., it can be
> doubted how much 'choice' women have about their decision to work only
> in the home.[50]

According to Joan Williams, the dominant culture shapes a "hegemony" of "values, norms, perceptions, and beliefs" that determines acceptable and unacceptable social alternatives.[51]

According to Susan Okin, what makes the homemaker choice problematic is that women often feel forced to make it. Okin argues that many times women make choices about their careers and families—such as to be primary parents or to treat their jobs as less important than their husband's—not because they affirmatively want to do so, but because they feel pressured to. Okin, in response to Kathleen Gerson's finding that women see themselves as confronting a choice between domesticity or career,[52] explains:

> Given the pervasiveness of sex-role socialization . . . the actual obstacles
> that our social structures place in the way of working mothers, and the far
> greater responsibility, both psychological and practical, that is placed on
> mothers than on fathers for their children's welfare, it is not surprising that
> these women perceived a conflict between their own work interests and the
> interests of any children they might have.[53]

Okin also emphasizes that "a woman's typically less advantaged position in the work force and lower pay may lead her to choices about full-time motherhood and domesticity that she would have been less likely to make had her work life been less dead-ended."[54] In a similar vein Okin criticizes theorists—she calls them "human capital theorists"—who argue that women's decisions to provide the unpaid domestic labor in a family are unobjectionable because they are economically efficient.[55] Okin suggests that regardless of, or perhaps because of, the possible economic efficiency of these decisions for the family unit as a whole, these decisions are often not freely made. Argues Okin, "Human capital theorists, in perceiving women's job market attachment as a matter of voluntary choice, appear to miss or virtually to ignore the fact of unequal power within the family. Like normative theorists who idealize the family, they ignore potential conflicts of interest, and consequently issues of justice and power differentials *within* families."[56] She explains that "the decisions of married women about their participation in the job market, even when they *are* choices, may not be such simple or voluntary choices as human capital theory seems to imply."[57]

A related criticism is that women choose to be full-time homemakers out of a set of life options that looks very different from the set of options facing similarly situated adult men. Women and men still face very different choice sets concerning their family and career options. Women often feel both an obligation and a right to be a full-time or primary caregiver to their children and know that such a role is incompatible with many careers. Men may feel less of a strain between their family and career options, but they are also less likely to feel any obligation or right to be stay-at-home parents. Women's socialization toward gendered roles is reinforced by the gendered set of life paths and options that women are presented with. If women's choice sets looked more like men's, it is suggested, fewer women would choose to be full-time homemakers. Until women's choice to do so arises out of a nongendered choice set—that is, until men and women face the same set of life options—women's choices are not freely made.

Okin, for example, focuses on the either/or choice that many women feel they face between having a serious career and being parents. "Needless to say," according to Okin, "such a choice does not confront boys in their formative years. *They* assume—reasonably enough, given our traditions and present conditions and beliefs—that what is expected of them as husbands and fathers is that, by developing a solid work life, they will provide the primary financial support of the family."[58] Okin reaffirms that it is not simply the case that women face an either/or choice set involving career and family while men face a choice set of career and family, but that women's and men's choice sets are substantively different with respect to what these options look like. She explains:

> Men's situation can have its own strains, since those who feel trapped at work cannot opt for domesticity and gain as much support for this choice as a woman can. . . . But boys do not experience the dilemma about work and family that girls do as they confront the choices that are crucial to their educations, future work lives and opportunities, and economic security.[59]

Okin argues that women's and men's different choices about career and family must be understood in light of the different choice sets out of which each group's choices arise. She points out:

> Socialization and the culture in general place more emphasis on marriage for girls than for boys. . . . This fact, together with their expectation of being the parent primarily responsible for children, clearly affects women's decisions about the extent and field of education and training they will pursue, and their degree of purposiveness about careers.[60]

Similarly, Williams argues that women's decisions to become full-time homemakers cannot be considered freely made when women and men face such different career and family choice sets and when only women are encouraged to pursue the choice of full-time homemaker. Williams argues:

> Feminists need to arm women to resist the argument that women's economic marginalization is the product of their own choice. Challenging this argument should be easy, since, in fact, in our deeply gendered system men and women face very different choices indeed. Whereas women, in order to be ideal workers, have to choose not to fulfill their "family responsibilities," men do not.[61]

Another common justification feminists offer for challenging the legitimacy of women's choices to be full-time homemakers focuses not on the conditions under which the choice is made—whether the choice was free enough—but on the future vulnerability such a choice may bring about.

Feminists most often argue that the homemaker choice renders women economically vulnerable upon the dissolution of their marriage by death or divorce. Women who leave the labor force, even if they intend the leave to be temporary, diminish their earning capabilities and may find it difficult to re-enter the labor market. The economic vulnerability argument takes on several different variations. First, feminists argue that a woman who chooses to become a full-time homemaker will both lower her earning potential and earn less over the course of her lifetime than she would if she did not leave the paid labor force. According to Reva Landau, "dropping out has a permanent effect on women's income even when they return to the labor force. . . . But, in view of the fact that women already have low incomes, they cannot afford to take actions that will further reduce this low income."[62] Joan Williams issues a similar warning:

> Today, many women with children continue to make choices that marginalize them economically in order to fulfill those same responsibilities, through part-time work, "sequencing," the "mommy track" or "women's work." In each case, the career patterns that accommodate women's child-care responsibilities often are ones that hurt women's earning potential.[63]

Second, feminists argue that a woman who becomes a full-time home-maker is likely to suffer a sharp and sudden decline in her standard of living upon the dissolution of her marriage. For example, Williams argues that "while women are keeping their side of the gender bargain, by 'choosing' to marginalize themselves economically in order to allow their husbands to perform as ideal workers, many men are no longer honoring their commitment to support their mates and children."[64] Williams cautions that women who choose to enter traditional gendered marriages and forgo paid employment often suffer impoverishment of both themselves and their children when the marriage ends.[65] Landau issues a similar caution. She admonishes feminists not to treat full-time homemaking as a valid career choice for women. "We are not doing anyone a favor by encouraging women to make the choice to work only in the home. We are encouraging a decision that hurts them, hurts their children, and hurts other women."[66]

Conclusion

The choices discussed in this chapter have generated a great deal of criticism by feminists. This criticism has most often taken the form of a narrow range of arguments focusing on the adequacy or fairness of the conditions under which the choices are made. Choices constrained by violence, socialization, and poverty are all challenged as not being made under adequate or fair conditions. Legitimate choices are those made under a fair social framework: one in which individuals choose their ends freely from an adequate range of options.

Feminists' focus on the fair framework is seemingly both liberal and neutral. The fair framework encourages individuals to freely choose their own ends. Perfectionism, which will be discussed more fully in the next chapter, provides an alternative ground for challenging the choices discussed in this chapter. Perfectionism is a theory of the good that talks directly about ends. Choices are criticized not because of the conditions under which they were made but because of the substance of the choices and their compatibility with human flourishing. Certain choices and activities are considered valuable or degrading for individuals regardless of how or why the choices were made.

3   An Introduction to Perfectionism

In contrast to liberalism's focus on social rights and fair conditions, perfectionism focuses directly on how people should live. Perfectionism, broadly defined, is a theory of the good life. According to Thomas Hurka, perfectionist theory "starts from an account of the good human life, or the intrinsically desirable life. . . . Certain properties, it says, constitute human nature or are definitive of humanity—they make humans humans. The good life, it then says, develops these properties to a high degree or realizes what is central to human nature."[1] Perfectionist theories divide into those arguing that certain activities and traits are inherently valuable—valuable in light of human nature—and those arguing that certain activities and traits are intrinsically valuable—valuable regardless of human nature. Vinit Haksar describes these views as weak and strong perfectionism. According to Haksar, weak perfectionism asserts that some forms of human life are superior to others because they "are more suited to human beings." In contrast, strong perfectionism says there are x's and y's such that "whatever human nature turns out to be . . . it would still be the case that x would be superior to y."[2]

Perfectionist theories provide a distinct alternative to the seemingly neutral procedural arguments that dominate feminist debates about women's choices. Rather than discussing whether choices were made under free or constrained choice conditions, perfectionist theories focus on what choices mean in themselves or what they mean in relation to human nature. Perfectionist theories abandon liberalism's neutrality toward ends by adopting substantive conceptions of human flourishing. Perfectionist theorists then criticize choices based on the degree to which the choices promote such human flourishing. Perfectionist theories are both moral and political. They describe what the good life looks like for the individual, and they encourage social policies and structures that promote individual flourishing.

In this chapter I present what seem to me to be the four most complete and thorough contemporary perfectionist theories. I present these theories in order to suggest perfectionism's potential to articulate a more honest basis for feminists' criticism of women's choices. I also show how the current perfectionist theories fail to live up to this potential.

In section I, I present the perfectionisms of Joseph Raz, Thomas Hurka, and George Sher. While these theories are derived from different starting points, they are all too abstract to be useful in guiding people's lives.

In section II, I present the perfectionism of Martha Nussbaum. While Nussbaum provides more specific requirements for human flourishing, her focus on the need for primary goods, which individuals living in industrialized societies already possess (or at least possess an agreed-upon social right to), renders her theory not very useful for women in these countries.

I. Abstract Perfectionisms

Joseph Raz puts forth a two-stage perfectionist theory. The first stage asserts the intrinsic value of autonomy and an autonomous life. The second stage modifies and narrows this perfectionism by stating that a good life is not simply one in which an individual is autonomous but one in which an individual autonomously chooses only "valuable" life choices. Unfortunately, Raz does not describe the criteria that render choices valuable and gives little guidance as to which choices these are.

Raz begins *The Morality of Freedom* by stating that his book "denies the revisionist approach and affirms the intrinsic value of liberty."[3] By this, Raz means that he denies that autonomy is valuable only instrumentally as a means to realizing other truly valuable ends such as justice, equality, or identified social rights.[4] Raz argues that autonomy is valuable in itself.[5]

While Raz does not explain why autonomy is intrinsically valuable, he does describe the conditions necessary for its existence. According to Raz, autonomy requires that an individual possess the mental abilities necessary to form intentions, develop complex plans, and connect means with their probable ends.[6] The individual must not only possess these cognitive rational capacities but must also have the physical capacities to exercise them meaningfully in constructing her day-to-day life. In order to be able to meaningfully exercise these physical and mental abilities, she needs to also have available an adequate range of plausible options to choose among, free from external coercion and manipulation.[7] Autonomous choices are those made under such conditions.

Raz's perfectionism, however, does not simply require that individuals live autonomously but that they direct their lives toward valuable ends. According to Raz, autonomy is only valuable to the extent that one chooses good options. Freely choosing good life paths and projects promotes human flourishing, but freely choosing bad life paths and projects does not. "Since autonomy is valuable only if it is directed at the good it supplies no reason to provide, nor any reason to protect worthless let alone bad options. . . . [W]hile autonomy is consistent with the presence of bad options, they contribute nothing to its value."[8] For Raz, it is not enough that an individual's actions are autonomous; they must also be valuable.

Clarifying what choices are valuable and why is the key to making Raz's theory practically useful. It is also where his theory is wholly inadequate. For example, Raz explains that certain kinds of intimate personal relationships are valuable because they involve the mutual recognition of each individual's unique subjectivity. According to Raz, "significant social forms, which delineate the basic shape of the projects and relationships which constitute human well-being, depend on a combination of incommensurability with a total refusal to even consider exchanging one incommensurate option for another."[9] Certain valuable social forms, like intimate personal relations and parental relations, can only exist if people recognize that the social relations are incommensurable with other kinds of market goods.[10] Raz emphasizes:

> Certain judgments about the non-comparability of certain options and certain attitudes to the exchangeability of options are constitutive of relations with friends, spouses, parents, etc. Only those who hold the view that friendship is neither better nor worse than money, but is simply not comparable to money or other commodities, are *capable* of having friends. Similarly, only those who would not even consider exchanges of money for friendship are capable of having friends.[11]

Individuals who learn to put a price on every kind of human association will lose the capacity to form and be part of these special kinds of interpersonal relationships.[12]

While this explains why some relationships are more valuable than others, it does not give much guidance as to how individuals should live their lives. Certainly not all one's interactions and relationships are of this intimate and incommensurable kind. Probably the bulk of the relationships one participates in each day are more functional and fungible business and commercial relationships. Individuals are seen and treated as instrumental means, not as unique ends in themselves. Raz suggests that a life in which all one's relationships are of this sort is degraded. But is it possible to have some instrumental relationships without degrading one's more valuable relationships? Or are some forms of instrumental relationships, like prostitution or slavery, so degraded that they cannot coexist with the more elevated forms of intimate relations? For example, is it possible for a woman to be a prostitute and still be able to maintain her more valuable relationships in which she is seen and treated as a nonfungible unique whole? Raz is helpful in describing why certain relationships are more valuable than others, but he does not say what this means for people's everyday lives.

The only other guidance Raz offers for distinguishing valuable from nonvaluable activities is an extremely brief list. The arts and monogamous marriage are, according to Raz, valuable, while hunting is either less valuable or not valuable at all.[13] Presumably monogamous marriage is valuable because it involves intimate mutual recognition. Raz, however, offers no explanation for what makes art valuable and hunting less so. Is Nazi art really more valuable than survival hunting? Raz does not explain what makes these specific activities valuable, and he therefore offers us no tools for evaluating the value of other activities.

Raz recognizes that the abstraction of his theory prevents it from providing practical guidance to society and individuals about what traits and activities should be encouraged. Raz's abstraction and vagueness about details and application is deliberate. Raz explains at the outset of *The Morality of Freedom:* "Though the ideas to be canvassed will presuppose certain views concerning the nature and working of society, these will largely remain in the background. Though the conclusions I will reach have implications for various political problems such as the control of immigration, censorship and taxation, the implications will not be spelt out."[14] Raz's goal is to argue for perfectionism as a theoretical alternative to liberalism rather than to describe his particular perfectionism's practical application. While Raz argues that perfectionism has great potential for directing individual and social decision making, ultimately, he chooses not to take on this challenge with his own theory.

Strangely, while Raz skimps on the details of his perfectionism, he provides more details about how society should promote it. Raz imposes obligations on individuals and the state to ensure that the internal and external conditions necessary for individual autonomy are met. According to Raz, "Autonomy-based duties . . . require the use of public power to promote the conditions of autonomy, to secure an adequate range of options for the population."[15]

Raz describes the forms that social promotion of perfectionist goals should take. According to Raz, "Conferring honours on creative and performing artists, giving grants or loans to people who start community centres, taxing one kind of leisure activity, e.g., hunting, more heavily than others, are all cases in which political action in pursuit of conceptions of the good falls far short of the threatening popular image of imprisoning people."[16]

Raz also endorses a vision of the harm principle that is more substantive than that put forth by John Stuart Mill and that obligates society to protect a richer version of autonomy. Mill's harm principle requires that the government not infringe on the freedom of any individual except to prevent that person from infringing on the autonomy of another individual.[17] Mill's harm principle focuses on protecting individuals' negative liberty from direct intrusions and coercion. Raz's harm principle is far more expansive and focuses on protecting and promoting individuals' positive liberty.

Individuals infringe upon the autonomy of another individual both by blocking action the individual would otherwise take and by not facilitating a range of options she might wish to act upon. According to Raz's harm principle, the government has a right to require individuals to promote others' autonomy in the second affirmative, enabling, sense. Raz's harm principle permits the government to prevent individuals from coercing others but also permits the government to require individuals to facilitate and promote another's autonomy. Raz describes the affirmative obligation his harm principle places on the government as such: "[I]f the government has a duty to promote the autonomy of people the harm principle allows it to use coercion both in order to stop people from actions which would diminish people's autonomy and in order to force them to take actions which are required to improve people's options and opportunities."[18]

Governments have an obligation to promote autonomy and are entitled to do so through economic redistribution, the provision of public goods, and making certain social services compulsory.[19] According to Raz, the government may coerce compliance with laws that are designed to promote the autonomy of its members because failure to comply with such laws harms others, thereby satisfying the harm principle and justifying the coercion.[20]

The outline for implementing Raz's theory is clear: the state may use a range of means to promote valuable autonomy among its citizens because an autonomous life lived in pursuit of valuable ends represents human flourishing. The details of Raz's perfectionism, however, are absent. Raz does not offer practical or theoretical guidance as to what options are valuable and "morally acceptable" and what options are not.[21] Individuals and the state are left not knowing what kinds of choices and activities they should or must encourage.

Thomas Hurka's amoral perfectionism puts him directly at odds with Raz's distinctly moral perfectionism focusing on valuable life choices. Hurka's theory is both internally focused and morally directionless—a combination that renders it even less useful for practical application than Raz's perfectionism.

Hurka starts from the premise that a good human life is one which develops "human nature" to a "high degree."[22] His first challenge, therefore, is to determine what constitutes "human nature." Hurka rejects two conceptions as inadequate. First, he rejects the notion that human nature can be equated with the properties "distinctive" of humans. He argues that there are many characteristics distinctive to humans that are also repulsive and not worthy of development, such as making destructive fires, despoiling the environment, and killing for fun.[23] Second, he rejects the notion that human nature can be equated with the properties "essential" to humans. Hurka argues such a conception reduces to a biological theory that includes many trivial characteristics, like taking up space and being "self-identical."[24]

The compound view of human nature Hurka ultimately settles on, the "essence-and-life view,"[25] avoids the theoretical flaws of the previous two conceptions but does not do much more practical work. "The best perfectionism . . . equates human nature with the properties essential to humans and conditioned on their being living things."[26] For example, according to Hurka, rationality is essential to what it means to be a living human. "We do not think there were humans in the world until primates developed with sufficient intelligence. . . . If we imagine a species with no capacity for a mental life, or with none more sophisticated than other animals', we do not take ourselves to be imagining humans."[27]

Hurka tries to give his perfectionism substance by describing three values that embody it: physical perfection, theoretical rationality, and practical rationality.[28] According to Hurka, physical perfection comes when each system in our body is performing its characteristic activity well. Basic physical perfection comes from good bodily health: "when all our bodily systems function in an efficient, unrestricted way."[29] Higher physical perfection comes from vigorous bodily activity such as exercise and athletics: "Here our major physical systems perform to higher degrees, processing more air, carrying more nutrients, and moving greater weights longer distances."[30] Rational perfection comes from the development and exercise of humans' capacities to form and act on sophisticated beliefs and intentions. Theoretical rationality focuses on individuals' ability to ground beliefs in evidence. Practical rationality focuses on individuals' ability to derive and direct acts from these beliefs and intentions.[31]

In effect, Hurka's expanded description of human perfection merely replaces one abstract conception of human perfection with three abstract conceptions of it. Hurka's perfectionism focuses on vague inner states rather than outward decisions or activities. Hurka provides little information about what conditions are required for the development of these inner states or how one knows when they are achieved.

Determining when rationality is being exercised is nearly impossible. How can one tell if an individual's life choices are the result of theoretical and practical rationality or the result of random choice? For example, one woman may prostitute herself because after a careful weighing of her other job opportunities and her short- and long-term goals and priorities, it best satisfies her needs. Another woman may prostitute herself because she has lived on the street since she was a teenager and does not know of any other way to support herself. Prostitution is the only way she can think of to support herself. It is hard to decipher these two women's decisions and activities from the outside looking in. Yet, the first woman's decision seems far more in keeping with Hurka's conception of human flourishing than does the second woman's.

Determining when choices promote or discourage the development of rationality is similarly difficult. For one seventeen-year-old the decision to drop out of high school—with no plans for the future and no prospects of employment—may be detrimental to the development of her rational capacities. For another seventeen-year-old the decision to drop out of high school—to pursue her computer software business full-time—may be perfectly in keeping with the development of her rational capacities.

Because it focuses on internal capacities, Hurka's theory does not offer any justification for criticizing choices from the outside. Hurka's theory might justify questioning an individual to see how and why a particular decision was made, but it does not justify challenging choices outright. That is, it cannot justify challenging all choices of a particular type, for example, all choices to prostitute oneself or all choices to leave the workforce. Hurka recognizes the problems with trying to socially encourage or legislate such an internal perfectionist vision. He notes that "[i]f perfection did not involve inner states, laws requiring it directly might be enforceable."[32]

The practical usefulness of Hurka's perfectionism is also undermined by its amoralism. Hurka does not endeavor to tell individuals what choices or activities are valuable and what life paths are better than others. Hurka, unlike Raz, argues on behalf of a nonmoralistic conception of human flourishing. His perfectionism is based on the development of human nature and the capacities that are essential to being human. But, Hurka argues, this development is just as valuable if done in an immoral as a moral direction.[33] The focus of perfectionism for Hurka is on the development and exercise of certain human traits and capacities, not on the direction or manifestation of the exercise. According to Hurka, "the best perfectionism must be free of [moralism]. It must never characterize the good by reference to conventional moral rules, but always non-morally; and in defending its claims about essence, it must likewise appeal only to non-moral considerations."[34] In practice this means, for the purposes of human flourishing, a person is just as well-off if she directs her creative genius toward finding a cure for cancer as if she directs it toward finding a more efficient way to spread the disease.

Hurka's perfectionism has practical use only in that it encourages the development of individuals' physical and intellectual capacities. Hurka argues the government should promote the perfection of its citizens through education aimed at ensuring that they develop their capacities for theoretical and practical rationality.[35] Hurka suggests the government should subsidize and encourage activities like literature, music, and athletics, and discourage or ignore activities like drug taking or professional wrestling.[36] The education system, and presumably the larger system of state subsidies and taxation, should "lay the foundations for valuable activities, not for ones of minimal worth."[37]

Hurka's perfectionism is limited to advocating the development of physical and cognitive capacities. He deliberately does not provide any guidance for how individuals should exercise these capacities and how they should direct their lives. His perfectionism, therefore, is not useful for the task of criticizing choices based on the nature of the choices alone.

George Sher is probably the vaguest of the theorists in offering specific applications of his perfectionist principles. Sher's vagueness is ironic since Sher makes the strongest claims about the practical effect his perfectionism is meant to have on social organizing.[38]

Sher is more forthright and ambitious than either Raz or Hurka in his claims about the political effect perfectionism should have. He promises his readers that he will put forth both a perfectionist theory of the traits and activities that are inherently valuable and an argument about the demands and obligations his perfectionism puts on political actors.[39] Sher argues that "once perfectionist considerations are admitted at all, they can be expected to play a role in many areas of political decision making."[40] According to Sher, perfectionist considerations are "relevant to decisions about public assistance, educational policy, the criminal and civil justice system, the prison system, city planning and land use, transportation policy, the tax code, support for cultural institutions, regulation of the entertainment industry, investment incentives, and the structure of institutions such as the military."[41] Unfortunately, Sher's perfectionism does not contain sufficient detail to direct social policy in any of these areas.

For Sher, human flourishing comes from the development of fundamental human capacities. Sher initially determines which capacities are fundamental by asking which characteristics are nearly universal and nearly inescapable for all persons. After uncovering these capacities Sher sets out to discover the telos of these capacities—the end toward which these capacities aim. According to Sher, human perfection is achieved by the development of fundamental human capacities to their natural end.[42] Sher's perfectionism is objective and teleological.[43] His theory of the good is not based on the development and pursuit of traits and activities that bring individuals subjective happiness but on the pursuit of traits and activities that develop fundamental capacities toward their particular goals.

Sher identifies three fundamental capacities that are, in accordance with his schema, nearly inescapable and nearly universal. They are theoretical rationality, practical rationality, and social interaction.[44] The goals of these capacities are, respectively, knowledge, rational activity, and mutual recognition.[45]

According to Sher, "each of us has both a native capacity to understand the world and an inescapable tendency to try to exercise that capacity."[46] The goal toward which we inescapably aim in exercising our rational capacities is knowledge and the truth of the questions that engage us.[47] Even if we try to avoid all truth seeking, "our success is temporary at best."[48] Sher concludes that knowledge must be a part of human perfection since it is the telos of a fundamental capacity. He explains that "if what has inherent value is the successful exercise of fundamental capacities, it would be very surprising if reason-based true belief—or, in other words, knowledge—were not inherently good."[49]

Similarly, no individual can avoid thinking about how to act in the world, and the goal of this practical rationality is rational activity.[50] According to Sher, "basing one's decision on one's weightiest combination of reasons is the *generic aim* of all practical deliberation."[51] "As practical agents, we are unavoidably implicated in a complex sequence of activities whose goal and characteristic tendency are the performance of reason-based actions."[52] Sher concludes: "[J]ust as knowledge belongs on our list of inherent goods, the formation and execution of reason-based plans . . . appear to belong there too."[53]

Sher's third fundamental capacity is that of forming and sustaining social bonds.[54] Sher acknowledges that the capacity to form and sustain social bonds seems less inescapable and less universal than our capacities for theoretical or practical deliberation. He argues though that over the long term "our efforts to form social bonds do seem close to inescapable. At the very least, we all have very powerful urges to seek out, communicate with, and care for and be cared for by other human beings."[55]

Sher argues that the goal of social interaction is mutual recognition and social identity. "Each person defines himself through the eyes of others. To regard ourselves as persons in the full sense, we must recognize others as recognizing us as rational and affective agents with a perspective of our own."[56] Sher makes clear that although mutual respect is the goal of social interaction, not all forms of social interaction are equally successful in achieving the goal. Friendships or romantic relationships between people who care for and respect each other are far more successful at achieving mutual recognition than are "interpersonal relations that are (e.g.) manipulative, exploitative, coercive, or destructive."[57]

In addition to the three fundamental capacities and their perfectionist goals, Sher argues that there are several other traits and activities that are derivative goods because they are useful or essential for achieving the telos of the fundamental capacities.[58] Sher identifies three such derivative goods: the development of one's abilities, moral goodness, and the appreciation of true beauty.[59] The derivative goods do not themselves satisfy Sher's schema of being nearly universal and nearly unavoidable fundamental capacities. Instead they derive their value as human goods from their connection to the development and satisfaction of the fundamental goals.[60]

Most broadly, Sher argues on behalf of the development of one's individual abilities, or at least the development of those abilities that will help one achieve one's fundamental goals. Sher explains that the development of a whole range of human abilities is necessary for achieving one's fundamental goals of knowledge, practical activity, and mutual social recognition. According to Sher, "almost every successful attempt to achieve a fundamental goal relies on, and would be impossible if the agent lacked, many previously developed abilities."[61] While Sher recognizes that the development of our abilities is not a fundamental capacity because it is "not a goal that we *do* near-universally and near-unavoidably pursue," he explains that "it is a goal that we *should* all pursue because of its relation to other goals that *are* near-universal and near-unavoidable."[62]

Sher clarifies that this derivative-value argument counsels for developing only those capacities that will contribute to the achievement of fundamental goals; it does not argue in favor of developing any and all possible human abilities. Which abilities should be developed because of their derivative value, Sher argues, is not hard to discern. Individuals should develop whichever abilities will contribute most to the achievement of their fundamental goals, and this determination "depends partly on the general usefulness of different skills and partly on the details of each agent's (past and future) aims and projects."[63]

In addition to the derivative-value argument for developing one's abilities, Sher puts forth two very similar arguments about the derivative value of moral goodness and aesthetic awareness. The value of both of these goods derives from their usefulness in helping one achieve the fundamental goal of rational activity.

The end of practical rationality is to identify and act in accordance with the best and strongest rationales available. According to Sher, moral reasons are often the best and strongest reasons for doing something. An agent must therefore appreciate moral goodness, or be possessed of moral goodness, in order to recognize and give proper weight to these moral values.[64] Following his assumption that moral reasons are significant, Sher explains that "if moral reasons *are* always very weighty, then no deliberating agent can fully achieve his generic aim without *assigning* them great weight."[65]

The argument on behalf of aesthetic awareness is parallel. Sher argues that like moral goodness, aesthetic value often provides very weighty reasons for acting in a particular way. Therefore, in order to achieve practical rationality, an agent must recognize and give due weight to aesthetic considerations.[66]

Sher, however, does not give specific examples of the kinds of activities that promote knowledge, of the activities that encourage or reflect practical rationality, or of the kinds of relationships that seem most likely to provide mutual recognition.[67] Sher does not explain whether high school or college graduation should be required in order to encourage knowledge, whether all adults should be required to earn their own income so that each individual will have the means to direct her own life, or whether prostitution should be discouraged or made illegal because it is incompatible with mutual recognition. Ultimately, Sher's promises of political and social applicability fall flat because of his lack of detail about the kinds of activities that in practice develop fundamental capacities to their natural ends. Like Raz and Hurka, Sher puts forth a theory of human flourishing that is appealing in the abstract but difficult to apply to concrete situations.

Ultimately, these three theories are similar in theory and inadequate in practice. The three theories envision similar kinds of intellectual development as required for human flourishing. For example, Hurka and Sher both argue that human flourishing requires theoretical rationality. For Sher this theoretical rationality must be aimed at knowledge, while for Hurka the theoretical rationality requires the ability to form beliefs, whether true or not, based on evidence. The capacity to understand different life options and to form beliefs and preferences based on them is also required by Raz's endorsement of valuable autonomy. In order to act upon the rational plans one has made for one's life, one must first form beliefs about what paths and projects are worthwhile. The cognitive capacities to form and justify one's beliefs seem to be essential to all three theorists' conceptions of human flourishing.

Similarly, all three theorists agree that human flourishing requires the development of something that looks like practical rationality. While Hurka and Sher openly state that the good human life requires practical rationality, it is clear that Raz's requirement of the exercise of valuable autonomy is also closely related to practical rationality. Raz's autonomy requires that in order to direct their life paths individuals be aware of and be able to weigh and compare the effect different choices will have on their lives. This ability to evaluate and act upon choices in a self-directed and purposeful manner is the same capacity required by practical rationality.

Both Raz and Sher also suggest that human flourishing requires, or at least is enhanced by, certain kinds of intimate personal relations. Sher's claim is stronger as he requires certain kinds of intimate, caring, and nonmanipulative interpersonal relationships in order for individuals to achieve the fundamental goal of personal recognition by others. Raz's claim is a bit weaker. He makes clear that certain valuable social forms such as friendship and intimate relations require that individuals treat themselves, others, and their relationships as noncommodifiable and incommensurable goods. It is less clear for Raz whether these kinds of social interactions are necessary for a meaningful human life or whether they are just one example among many of a valuable life choice. In either case, both theories place significant emphasis on the importance of intimate interpersonal relations for a good human life.

Because of their abstraction, the theories are all similarly difficult to apply. Does the perfectionist ideal of theoretical rationality counsel in favor of mandatory public education past the age of sixteen to ensure that individuals develop the cognitive skills necessary to absorb and process information about the world? Does the need to develop and maintain the capacities for theoretical rationality counsel against individuals dropping out of public-sphere activities as adults? One might argue that the way that individuals develop and maintain their capacities for theoretical rationality in our culture is first through the formal education process and later in life through their participation in the public sphere of paid or voluntary employment. Participating with other groups and individuals in the public sphere is the way individuals receive their most salient information about their fellow citizens and hone their skills of abstract thinking. In our complicated and impersonal society, it may be that the best way for individuals to develop and maintain the necessary skills to think about abstract issues of social justice and economic distribution is by interacting with many other different kinds of people in the public sphere.

The goal of theoretical rationality may, therefore, counsel in favor of certain career choices and against others. In practical terms, the ideal of theoretical rationality may mean that individuals should be encouraged to remain public-sphere participants throughout their lives and should be discouraged from removing themselves from such activities and sequestering themselves among family and friends.

The theories discussed, of course, give no such suggestions about what the ideal of theoretical rationality means in terms of people's real lives. None of the theorists discussed wants to descend from the safety of theory into the controversial murkiness of everyday life to say that being a philosopher is better than being a homemaker. While such avoidance certainly makes the theories less controversial and less offensive than they would otherwise be, it also makes them less useful.

Similarly, although all three theorists suggest a perfectionist ideal of practical rationality—the ability to direct the course of one's life in accordance with one's beliefs—they offer scant guidance as to how the goal of practical rationality should affect individual or social decision making. Does practical rationality require that an individual, in addition to having the internal capacities for theoretical rationality, also have certain external capacities to materially direct and guide her life in accordance with the plan she has formulated for herself? Would then an ideal of practical rationality applied in a society such as our own counsel in favor of decisions that give an individual a certain degree of social and financial power so that she has an adequate array of meaningful options available and the material wherewithal to direct her life in the ways she desires?[68]

Even prior to questions about material well-being, might the ideal of practical rationality actually require a certain level of self-love and self-esteem on the part of all individuals? Is a level of self-love necessary to enable people to even conceptualize themselves as individuals worthy of having their own aims and projects and as individuals able to direct their life paths in accordance with their plans?

The perfectionist ideal of practical rationality might have real things to say about individuals' decisions to enter the workforce or to become financially dependent upon another individual. It may also have social-policy implications for how a society should socialize its children, how seriously it should take problems like domestic violence, and how it should encourage its citizens to divide paid and unpaid labor within families.

Raz and Sher also argue that a good human life includes certain kinds of social interactions and relationships. The theorists discuss the value of relationships that are free of manipulation, exploitation, and commodification. Raz focuses on the need for friendships and intimate relationships devoid of market concerns. Sher focuses on the importance of relationships based on mutual caring and respect so that individuals feel recognized and appreciated for themselves.

As with theoretical rationality and practical rationality, it is unclear how the perfectionist ideal of certain kinds of interpersonal relations would play out with respect to the actual decisions people face. If mutually caring intimate relationships are important, or required, for human flourishing, does this mean that individuals cannot live meaningful lives if they commodify their sexuality and take part in noncaring but physically intimate relationships? Does the importance of mutually caring relationships bar people from having commodified relationships, or can an individual have both kinds, even if only the first contributes to human flourishing? If commodified sexual relations prevent individuals from being capable of forming the kind of intimate personal relations necessary for human flourishing—because they lose the ability to think of themselves or others in the appropriate way—then what kinds of commodified activities must be discouraged? Should individuals be discouraged only from the most crass form of sexual commodification—prostitution—or must they also be discouraged from other variations of sexual commodification—stripping, pornographic modeling, fashion modeling? Where does the perfectionist ideal of caring intimate relations come down on these real-life choices and why?

In his praise of Raz's work, Jeremy Waldron defends the high level of abstraction of Raz's perfectionism. Waldron asks: "Does it matter that Raz says almost nothing about what makes an option or an individual's conceptions of the good repugnant or immoral, even though the central thrust of his argument is to establish the government's right, indeed its duty, to extirpate options of this sort?"[69] Waldron concludes that "perfectionism is better defended without examples."[70]

Waldron and Raz are certainly right that there is a value in discussing theoretical ideals without getting stuck in the controversial morass of practical application. There is a value to discussing the merits of liberalism or perfectionism apart from their practical applications. Yet, in order for perfectionism to be a useful moral and political theory—one that provides guidance to people about how to structure their lives—perfectionism must be grounded and context-specific.

The vagueness of abstract theory has saved perfectionism from descending to the pedantic level of everyday problems. But it has also kept perfectionism from having any real usefulness for individuals trying to determine how best to live their lives and for societies trying to encourage individuals to live good lives.

II. Nussbaum's Concrete Perfectionism

In contrast to the abstract theories discussed above, Martha Nussbaum's perfectionism offers a concrete list of the internal capabilities and external conditions necessary for a good human life. Nussbaum's perfectionism, however, is wholly procedural. A good human life is one in which the individual has the capacity for various forms of essential human functioning, not one in which she necessarily utilizes these capacities. All choices made under conditions in which an individual possesses the capacities are acceptable; those made when the individual does not possess the requisite capabilities are subject to challenge.[71]

In a number of different articles Nussbaum establishes a fairly consistent list of the functional capabilities she sees as necessary for a fully human life. Nussbaum's list includes physical safety, the capacity for good health, and the ability to plan one's life and to act on this plan.[72]

Nussbaum recognizes that individual possession of the functional capabilities necessary for a good human life requires the development of certain internal conditions and the presence of certain external ones. Several of the capabilities on Nussbaum's list—for example, practical reason, a sense of relatedness to other individuals, and an ability to form a conception of the good—require the existence of particular cognitive and emotional skills that must be developed within the individual. Nussbaum calls these capabilities "I-capabilities" and describes them as "traits of intellect and character and body" that are "*internal*" to each person.[73] Nussbaum stresses that "I-capabilities are developed by education."[74]

Nussbaum's list also requires certain external conditions. Nussbaum recognizes that some external conditions, what she calls "E-capabilities," are necessary for the existence of I-capabilities.[75] Only if one has proper nutrition and adequate physical security, for example, can one exercise and develop one's internal capabilities for reason, empathy, and a sense of justice, and even for sociability and an ability to play.

For Nussbaum, the role of government is to ensure the existence of these essential capabilities in all individuals who are born with a basic, though undeveloped, capacity for them. The government must both ensure that individuals have the external resources required for the exercise of these capabilities and must foster their development. "[T]he legislator's total task will be to train I-capabilities in the young, to maintain those in the adult, and simultaneously to create and preserve the E-circumstances in which those developed capabilities can become active."[76] Nussbaum explains that the duty of government is to provide for and ensure these capabilities. "Government . . . is directed to make sure that all human beings have the necessary resources and conditions for acting in [certain valued] ways. It leaves the choice up to them."[77]

As the above quotation indicates, Nussbaum works hard to distinguish her perfectionism from outcome-oriented perfectionism by emphasizing that her requirement of capabilities does not extend into a requirement that one exercise those capabilities.[78] "The list is a list of capabilities, not a list of actual functions, precisely because the conception is designed to leave room for choice."[79] Nussbaum argues that the development of the capability of choice itself is one of the most central capabilities promoted by her vision of the good life. Hence, Nussbaum contends, her list of required capabilities promotes more meaningful reflective and autonomous choices. It does not constrict an individual's range of possible choices.[80]

Nussbaum's focus on conditions and capacities brings her perfectionism close to the fuzzy line between liberalism and perfectionism described in the introduction. Although Nussbaum is clear that she is putting forth a conception of human flourishing, her reluctance to actually require that individuals exercise certain cognitive capacities, rather than simply possess them, brings her perfectionism fairly close to the process-based value neutrality at the heart of liberalism. Moreover, Nussbaum's focus on the possession rather than the exercise of critical capacities is pragmatically problematic because it is not clear how one could be sure that a woman possessed the necessary capabilities for rationality and self-determination, for example, if she never actually exercised these capacities.

Nevertheless, Nussbaum's procedural perfectionism, unlike the abstract perfectionism of Raz, Hurka, and Sher, supplies a clear basis to challenge choices made by women who are deprived of certain essential human capabilities. However, while Nussbaum's perfectionism is useful for challenging the choices of women in underdeveloped countries whose deprivation, according to Nussbaum's list, is obvious, her perfectionism is far less useful for feminists attempting to criticize choices made by women in industrialized countries who do not suffer such obvious deprivation.

Nussbaum's perfectionism shows its force and power in the very arena for which she designed it, that of developing nations. Nussbaum's perfectionism allows her to criticize the deep deprivation of women in such countries. Nussbaum challenges the existence of menstruation taboos that restrict women's ability to choose and execute their own life plans and projects.[81] She argues on behalf of the introduction of the smallpox vaccination into India even at the risk of eradicating the cult of Sittala Devi, the goddess to whom one historically prayed to avoid smallpox, on the grounds that bodily health is required for human flourishing.[82]

Nussbaum challenges the legitimacy of choices women make under conditions of deprivation. Nussbaum advocates women's literacy projects in rural Bangladesh despite women's initial lack of interest in the programs. According to Nussbaum, one cannot meaningfully choose not to exercise a capability essential to human flourishing when one does not yet possess the capability.

Nussbaum recounts a literacy project directed and described by Martha Chen,[83] in which members of a development agency held to their conviction that literacy was an important basic good despite the village women's lack of interest.[84] Nussbaum praises Chen and the development workers for not giving up on their literacy campaign simply because the women did not respond to their initial distribution of literacy materials.[85] Instead, the development workers sought to evolve a new strategy involving women's cooperatives formed to convince the local women of the value and power of literacy and of its necessity for a good human life. The women gradually came to see the benefits and usefulness of literacy. Only this essentialist commitment to a shared humanity, argues Nussbaum, made this improvement in women's capabilities, and hence in the quality of their lives, possible.[86]

Nussbaum's focus on available capabilities rather than on actual choice outcomes, however, seems much less useful for criticizing choices made by American women who already possess the functional capabilities on her list. Nussbaum's procedural perfectionism neither provides feminists with much leverage to criticize American women's life choices nor offers much promise of social change were her perfectionism to be consciously adopted by policy makers.

Most Americans believe, and are probably right in believing, that the overwhelming majority of American women already possess the functional capabilities that Nussbaum describes. Most American women have access to adequate food and shelter and to some medical attention. Almost all Americans have received mandatory schooling until the age of sixteen and hence should have developed the capability to think, reason, form a conception of the good, and develop a plan for their own lives.[87] Furthermore, federal and state constitutions guarantee women a wide range of choices regarding their work lives, religious lives, and personal lives, free from interference.

Imagine a middle-class woman with a college education who quits her job as a company administrator in order to stay home with her newborn baby because she feels pressure from her friends or family to do so. It is hard to argue that she does not have the capability to do otherwise. Certainly she is able to work and participate in the public sphere, and certainly she is able to critically reflect on her life and form a life plan. She has been making choices from a range of options up until this point. It seems implausible at best, and patronizing at worst, to argue that this woman's choice to leave the paid workforce and stay home should be challenged because the woman does not possess the functional capabilities of reason, logic, and self-determinacy to do otherwise.

Consider also the case of a woman who becomes a pornographic model because it is the highest-paying work she can find. Simply because the woman cannot find more remunerative work does not mean that she can find no other work that will provide for her physical well-being. She could probably find work, albeit low-paying work, in a service-sector or manual-labor job. At worst, she might qualify to receive public assistance. The critical point is that the woman is able to provide for her physical well-being in other ways and is also able to form and act upon a conception of her life that does not involve pornographic modeling. Though the life options for poor women are narrow even in this country, it seems far too extreme to argue that these women are denied the capability to think, reason, and develop life plans for themselves. American women, even poor and badly educated ones, do have the ability to shape their lives in some ways and do have a range of job options, albeit low-paying ones, open to them.

Finally, imagine the decision of a female college student to have sex with her male professor in exchange for a better grade. Again, it seems to over-stretch the viability of Nussbaum's capability list to argue that the typical female college student lacks the capability to think reflectively and critically about the choice and to shape her life in a way that does not involve exchanging sex for an improved grade.

I can think of two strong arguments that could be made against my claims that Nussbaum's procedural perfectionism does not give feminists much leverage to criticize the types of American women's choices on which I am focusing. The first criticism is that I am seriously deluded about the rosy status enjoyed by most American women. There are many who enjoy neither physical safety, adequate nutrition, nor proper education. These women would certainly benefit from social adoption of Nussbaum's vision of human flourishing. The second criticism is that even if American women do have the resources, both external and internal, that would be deemed sufficient to pos-

sess Nussbaum's functional capabilities in some societies, those same resources may not be enough to ensure that an individual has these capabilities
in the United States. For example, it may require more in the way of education
and financial resources to be able to develop a plan for one's life in the United
States than it does for an individual to do the same in rural Bangladesh.

In response to the claim that I am painting too rosy a picture of American
women's lives, I agree that there are certainly women and men in the United
States who are kept from possessing the capabilities on Nussbaum's list. In
proclaiming Nussbaum's perfectionism inadequate for American feminism, I
am not arguing that Nussbaum's procedural perfectionism would never be
useful for American women or that its thorough adoption would not alter the
conditions of some individuals' lives. Certainly, the majority of girls who are
in prostitution today do not have the capability for good health, to avoid unnecessary pain, or to develop and enact their own life plans. Battered women
too are denied these capabilities, as are women who are forced into pornography. A deep endorsement of Nussbaum's capabilities list would challenge decisions made under such conditions and would require social policies aimed
at developing the needed capabilities.

I am arguing only that most American women do already possess the functional capabilities on Nussbaum's list, so that social endorsement of her procedural perfectionism would not encourage any change in their lives. Furthermore, the capabilities on Nussbaum's list are formally guaranteed for all
Americans so that their lack is already perceived as a problem and as a sign
of deprivation. The guarantee of such things as proper shelter and nutrition
as well as education and self-determination may be formal rather than actual,[88] but even the formal guarantee of such things means that there are ave-
nues in place by which to challenge circumstances of deprivation. Individuals
who are being beaten or who lack food and shelter or who have been denied
education do have some claim upon our government to protect their physical
integrity, to guarantee the basic necessities for human life, and to provide
them with a basic public education. Nussbaum's procedural perfectionism
and the choice critiques it justifies just do not get American women a richer
version of substantive equality than they already have.

I take the second criticism to mean that while learning to read and write
may be enough to provide an individual with the capability to plan and live
one's life in a small rural community in a nonindustrialized country, both
more and different skills are needed by American women. In contemporary
America, for example, one might need an understanding of computers, and
of the interconnectedness of America with the world economy. Although

American women may possess the external resources and the internal conditions necessary for a good life in rural Bangladesh, because of the demands of American society, these resources and conditions may not be sufficient to ensure American women the internal capabilities necessary for human flourishing within American society.

This argument is problematic because even if true, it does not justify feminist criticism of women's as opposed to men's choices. While it may be true that Americans require greater resources, primarily in the area of education, in order to develop the internal capabilities on Nussbaum's list, it seems difficult to argue that women are disproportionately disadvantaged in the receipt of these resources. Particularly when the graduation rates of women and men from high school and college are approximately equal,[89] it seems very hard to argue that women are disproportionately denied the education required to develop and exercise their capacity for practical reason. American women may be disproportionately discouraged from exercising their capacity for practical reason in certain ways—there are many fewer female physicists and surgeons than male ones—but this difference of outcome does not suggest that women are not exercising their capability for practical reason, much less that they are denied such a capability altogether. Thus, Nussbaum's perfectionism, to the extent it is useful in American society at all, is unable to challenge mainstream women's life choices that seem premised on largely the same formal resources as men's yet still perpetuate their weaker social status. It is too hard to argue that women in particular are disproportionately deprived of the physical resources and education needed to develop cognitive capabilities that are meaningful in American society.

Nussbaum's perfectionism, while less abstract than the others, is not too useful for American feminists because American women already possess in law, and also usually in fact, the primary goods and internal capacities required by Nussbaum's perfectionism. For a perfectionism to be useful to American women, it must move beyond a focus on the context and conditions under which choices are made to an open scrutiny of choices themselves.

Conclusion

The perfectionist theories outlined in this chapter provide a general introduction to perfectionist ideals and suggest an alternative justification for challenging choices to the neutral proceduralism that dominates contemporary feminist discourse. I have criticized the existing theories not for their inadequacy as ideal theories but for their inability to further my present task: to understand and justify feminist criticisms of certain choices women make. The abstract theories do not give enough guidance to challenge specific choices while the sole concrete theory does not give us guidance that is relevant to my target population. As will be argued in the coming chapters, feminist criticisms of women's choices can only be understood and justified by reference to a theory of human flourishing. That theory, however, must be richer and more specific than those seen so far.

Part Two. The Inadequacy of Nonperfectionist Choice Critiques

The first part of this book contrasted feminists' neutral-sounding criticisms of women's choices with perfectionist theories advocating particular visions of human flourishing. While the previous chapters attempted to take feminist arguments on their face and highlight their divergence from perfectionism, the following four chapters reveal that this is a false contrast. The feminists described in chapter 2 are engaged in a kind of bait and switch: using neutral language to make arguments that are, in fact, justifiable only by resort to perfectionist principles. The following chapters show the perfectionism hidden within feminists' arguments.

The next four chapters show how four specific neutral-sounding arguments actually rely on perfectionist principles. The chapters look at feminist choice critiques based on coercion, socialization, inequality of choice sets between women and men, and women's future vulnerability. Each chapter pushes a particular argument to its limit to see what choices it can criticize while remaining neutral toward conceptions of the good, and what choices it cannot. Each chapter shows that many of the choices feminists care most deeply about cannot be criticized if one remains truly neutral toward competing conceptions of the good. Throughout these chapters, I suggest that what really motivates and drives feminists' arguments is not a neutral commitment to freedom or equality but a perfectionist commitment to a particular, albeit inchoate, vision of human flourishing.

4 Coercion Critiques

This chapter compares society's traditional conception of coercion with many feminists' far more expansive use of the term. As shown in chapter 2, feminists describe many women's choices to sexually commodify themselves, sexually objectify themselves, and become full-time homemakers as forced, pressured, or coerced, in order to delegitimize the choices. The use of such coercion language is not surprising. Coercion arguments provide the simplest and most acceptable way to challenge the legitimacy and validity of an individual's choice. However, while traditional conceptions of coercion are narrowly prescribed and can be justified on neutral grounds, many choices feminists criticize using the language of coercion are not coerced in the traditional sense and can only be explained as problematic by adopting a far more expansive and perfectionist conception of coercion. This chapter identifies the perfectionism hidden in feminists' coercion-based criticisms of women's choices to commodify their sexuality, objectify their sexuality, and become full-time homemakers.

I. Traditional Conceptions of Coercion

Most typically, we say a person is coerced if she is forced to choose between performing some unwanted act and having her rights violated. For example, a person may choose a suboptimal option in order to avoid a threatened violation of some personal or property right to which the individual is entitled. Because individuals should not make choices solely in order to avoid rights violations, choices made under such circumstances are generally considered coerced and illegitimate.

Consider Mary, who as an initial baseline condition has the choice to run, skip, or jump, and she prefers the options in that order. Left on her own, Mary would choose to run. Assume, however, that Alex tells Mary that she must skip or he will hit her. In this case, Mary chooses to skip even though her preference ordering is clear and skipping is not her optimal choice. Mary's choice is coerced. In order to avoid being hit, she must select one of her less-preferred options.

Sometimes, however, we also say a choice is coerced if it was made in order to avoid some harm to an individual's existing level of well-being. For example, the threatened harm might not come in the form of physical abuse or destruction of property but might involve the loss of one's job or eviction from one's home. In this case, a person chooses a suboptimal option in order to avoid a harm to some existing level of well-being for which the individual has a legitimate expectation of stability.[1]

A. Threatened-Rights-Violation Version of Coercion

The legal system invalidates choices made in response to threats in a number of different ways depending upon both the choice made and the threat used to induce it. For example, the legal system may (1) criminalize coercion by prosecuting the coercer and holding invalid the coercee's submission, as in cases of extortion, rape, or robbery;[2] (2) excuse those whose actions would normally be sanctionable, as in cases of duress;[3] or (3) refuse to enforce contracts that are a product of coercion, as in cases of duress, or unconscionability.[4]

The rights-violation version of coercion identifies a baseline of entitlements such as physical integrity and private property. A choice is coerced when an individual does something she would not otherwise have chosen to do in order to avoid a relatively significant threatened rights violation. The classic example of a coerced choice is the one made in response to a mugger's demand of "your money or your life." The person who is given this choice and decides to hand over her wallet would, of course, prefer to remain in her original state in which she possesses both her money and her life. She is forced to choose a second-best option, having her life but not her money, in order to avoid her least-favored option, which entails a threatened rights violation, namely the loss of her life. The woman's choice is, however, illegitimate and nonbinding. If the police were to find the mugger and the woman's wallet, the wallet would still belong to the woman and would be returned to her. The woman's decision to give her wallet to the mugger in order to save her life was not a "real" choice and is not enforced.

In the eighteenth century, the law of duress only considered choices coerced and nonbinding if they were made in response to threats to one's physical person.[5] Gradually the law has come to recognize severe threats to one's property as also rendering a choice coerced.[6] For example, a storekeeper's choice to pay some weekly sum to an organized crime syndicate in order to avoid the destruction of her store would probably be considered a choice made under duress—and the shopkeeper a victim of extortion. She chooses to make the payoffs in order to avoid a severe violation of her rights.[7] The storekeeper would not be legally bound by her promise to pay the crime syndicate if she reneged on the promise once the most dangerous members of the organization were put in prison and she no longer felt a threat to her shop.

Robert Nozick offers an often repeated example of a rights-violation version of coercion involving a slave who is beaten each day by her owner. One day the owner proposes that he will not beat her if and only if she performs some specific task that is disagreeable to her.[8] This proposal constitutes a threat and the slave's decision to perform the disagreeable act rather than endure a beating is coerced since the choice was made in order to avoid a rights violation. Assume the slave's preference ordering is (1) not perform the disagreeable act and not be beaten; (2) perform the disagreeable act and not be beaten; (3) not perform the act and be beaten. The slave's choice of option 2 is coerced.[9] She chooses to perform the disagreeable task in order to avoid the violation of a right that she is considered, by us if not by her owner, to hold. It does not matter, according to the rights-violation version of coercion, that the owner violates the slave's moral baseline every day by beating her. All that is important for analyzing this particular decision is that the slave is performing an act she would prefer not to perform in order to avoid a consequence that she has a right not to suffer.

Consider a second example offered by Alan Wertheimer of a donor, Andy, who regularly gives a school a large annual contribution. The school has traditionally refused to admit women. This year Andy makes his contribution contingent upon the school's changing its policies and admitting women.[10] Under the rights-violation version of coercion, the school's decision to change its single-sex admissions policy is not coerced because it did not make the choice in order to avoid a rights violation. Suppose the school's preference ordering is (1) continue to receive Andy's donation with no conditions attached; (2) receive Andy's donation and change its single-sex admissions policy; (3) maintain its single-sex admissions policy and not receive the donation. The school may feel forced to choose option 2 in order to avoid the bad consequences of option 3, and it may think that it has no real choice. However, under the rights-violation version of coercion this choice is not coerced. The school does not have any right to continue receiving Andy's donation. Hence, the school's decision to change its admissions policy in order to avoid losing the donation is not coerced.

Consider a third example of a boy telling the girl he has been dating for several weeks that if she does not have sex with him he will break up with her.[11] Assume that the girl's preference ordering is (1) continue dating and not have sex; (2) have sex and continue dating; (3) not have sex and not continue dating. Although the girl may feel that she is being forced to have sex that she does not want to have in order to avoid her least-favored alternative, according to the rights-violation version of coercion, her decision to have sex with the boy in order to continue dating him is not coerced. The girl has no right to continue dating this boy on her condition of abstinence. She is not choosing a less-preferred option in order to avoid a rights violation. Instead, she is making a choice she would prefer not to make in order to avoid losing something that she wants but is not entitled to: the continued relationship with this boyfriend.

However, even if a choice is coerced in the traditional sense, this does not always free the decision maker from responsibility for the ramifications of the choice. What seems important to our intuitive determinations of when coercion absolves the decision maker of responsibility for a choice is not simply whether one makes the choice in order to avoid a threatened rights violation but also (1) how severe the threatened rights violation is; (2) how awful the act the agent does in order to avoid the threatened rights violation is; and (3) who or what is imposing the threat upon the agent.

For example, if Bob tells Alex: "Rob that 7-Eleven store or I will step on your foot," Alex's decision to rob the 7-Eleven in order to avoid this rights violation does not really seem blameless because the threatened violation is so minor. Most people would probably still want to hold Alex responsible for his decision in this circumstance. Likewise, if Bob tells Alex: "Kill three students or I will beat you up," Alex would probably not be absolved of responsibility for his actions in the same way that we absolve the woman who is mugged of responsibility for her choice to give over her wallet in order to avoid being beaten. Although both decision makers face the same fairly significant rights violation of being physically beaten, the harm caused by Alex's actions far exceeds that caused by the woman being mugged.[12] While both choices are technically coerced, we would probably still seek to hold Alex responsible for his coerced decision while not binding the woman to or holding her responsible for her decision to give her wallet to a mugger. Finally, imagine that Alex robs a convenience store. Bob finds out about it and tells Alex that he must either pay him $500 or go to jail. Some people might feel that Alex should not be bound by his decision to pay Bob the money because the decision was the product of extortion. However, probably no one would say that Alex is not really committed by his decision to pay money in order to avoid jail if the choice were given to Alex by a judge before whom Alex was standing for sentencing. Whether one views Alex as responsible for and bound to his choice seems to depend on the difference in authority of the person making the threat in the two scenarios.[13]

Despite these subtleties and many potential complexities, at its core the rights-based version of coercion defines a choice as coerced when it is made in response to a threatened rights violation. Because such a threat is illegal and immoral, the resulting choice is (often) considered void and nonbinding.

B. Threatened-Status-Quo-Violation Version of Coercion

A second version of coercion that begins to expand the traditional notion of coerced choices is based on threats to one's empirical level of well-being rather than on threats to specifically designated rights. This version of coercion challenges the validity of decisions made in order to avoid a threat to one's existing and relied-upon level of well-being. For example, the drug dealer who, in response to the demand "Pay me $500 or I'll hand you over to the police," decides to pay the $500 is acting under coercion according to this model.[14] Choices made in order to avoid a threatened violation of one's baseline condition of well-being may still be considered legally valid or enforceable. But the choices nonetheless are suspect and open to criticism because they do not reflect the decision maker's true preference ordering. Analyzing the scenarios presented for the rights-violation version of coercion will help make the status-quo-violation version of coercion more clear and will highlight the differences between the two versions.

Reconsider first Nozick's example of the slave who is beaten each day by her owner until one day the owner proposes that he will not beat her if she performs some specific task that is disagreeable to her.[15] As explained earlier, this proposal is considered coercive under the threatened-rights-violation version of coercion because every person has a right to be free from physical attack. Under the status-quo-violation version of coercion, however, the owner's proposal is not a coercive threat but simply an offer. If the test of whether a proposal is coercive is whether the person making the choice will be worse off than she is currently if she does not accept a particular option, then the slave is not being coerced to choose to perform the disagreeable task. If the slave chooses not to perform the task, she will be in the same position she was in before: undergoing daily beatings. The slave has more options than she did before the proposal. She can remain in her preproposal baseline state consisting of daily beatings or she can choose to perform the new task. The owner's proposal does not threaten to worsen the slave's baseline condition of well-being and hence is not considered coercive under the threatened-status-quo-violation version of coercion.

Second, reconsider Wertheimer's example of the financial donor who gives a large annual contribution to a school that has traditionally refused to admit women. This year the donor makes his donation contingent upon the school's admitting women.[16] Determining whether the donor's proposal is coercive and whether the school's decision to change its admissions policies was coerced depends upon what one considers to be the school's status quo baseline condition of well-being. Identifying this baseline is both the trickiest and most important part of the threatened-status-quo-violation version of coercion. Normally, one's baseline condition of well-being can be identified in several different ways, leading to different conclusions about whether a particular proposal is a coercive threat to one's well-being.

For example, if the school's baseline condition of well-being is defined as receiving the same annual contribution it has received in years past and expected for the future, then the donor's proposal threatens to worsen its status quo and is coercive according to that standard. The donor is forcing the school to do something it would not ordinarily choose to do, admit women, in order to maintain its baseline level of well-being. However, the school's baseline condition of well-being may also be that each year it receives various donations with various conditions attached to them and that it must decide either to meet the conditions and keep the donation or refuse the conditions and return the donation. If this position of fiscal uncertainty is taken as the school's baseline condition, then the donor's conditional pledge would not seem to be a threat to the school's well-being but simply a restatement of its normal position.

The third example, of the boy who tells the girl he has been dating for several weeks that he will break up with her if she does not have sex with him, also involves an ambiguous baseline condition. How one defines the girl's baseline condition of well-being determines whether her decision to have sex in order to avoid a breakup is considered coerced under the threatened-status-quo-violation version of coercion. If the girl's baseline condition of well-being is to continue dating the boy, then the boy's proposal of sex or a breakup threatens to worsen her baseline condition. Under this model, the girl is coerced to choose her less-preferred option of having sex in order to avoid destruction of her current level of well-being: dating this boy.

Suppose, however, the girl's baseline level of well-being is that she will date this boy only so long as both of them are satisfied with the relationship. Neither the girl nor the boy have any entitlement that the relationship will continue or that it will continue on terms suitable to one party only. If the girl's status quo baseline of well-being is this expectation of dating only so long as both parties are satisfied with the terms of the relationship, then the boy's proposal that they either have sex or break up does not threaten to worsen the girl's condition but again merely replicates it. Since the girl's baseline condition of well-being involves a conditional and unstable relationship with the boy, the boy's request to break up is not a threat to this baseline but merely an example of its instability.

This version of coercion is less clearly defined and more situation-specific than the rights-violation version. While liberal rights are agreed upon and constant across situations, an individual's baseline status of well-being is less clear and is wholly situation-specific. As the examples suggest, the status-quo-violation version of coercion is both broader and narrower than the rights-violation version of coercion, because its breadth is dependent to a considerable degree on how the status quo is defined.

C. Neutral Justifications of Traditional Conceptions of Coercion

The rights-violation version of coercion and, to a lesser extent, the status-quo-violation version are accepted and uncontroversial conceptions of coercion. These versions of coercion are uncontroversial because they can be justified without resort to perfectionist ideals. The rights-based version of coercion follows directly from the vesting of rights in individuals. To the extent that individuals possess rights, choices made in response to threatened violations of these rights must be invalid. Therefore, theories that justify the vesting of rights on neutral grounds also provide neutral justifications for the threatened-rights-violation version of coercion.

Both of the traditional versions of coercion can be explained by reference to neutral or very weakly perfectionist theories of political organization. For example, the threatened-rights-violation version of coercion can be justified on utilitarian, Kantian, conventionalist, or autonomy-enhancing grounds. The threatened-status-quo-violation version can be justified by conventionalism.

1. Utilitarian Justifications Both traditional utilitarianism and Richard Posner's theory of wealth maximization provide neutral justifications for the threatened-rights-violation version of coercion. These theories aim at maximizing some index of social welfare—for utilitarianism, happiness, and, for Posner, wealth—while remaining silent about how individual lives should be lived. The theories derive rights not from normative principles but from the principle of maximization itself. Neither theory endorses or encourages a vision of human flourishing. Without adopting a conception of the good, these theories are able to justify, albeit through rather self-serving and conclusory fundamental assumptions, the vesting of liberal rights in the individual and the subsequent invalidation of choices made in response to threatened rights violations.

The critical, though perhaps uncontroversial, assumption utilitarianism makes in order to justify vesting individuals with liberal rights is that people feel happiest when they know the state will protect their rights. As John Stuart Mill argues, the reason society should defend people's possession of rights is "general utility."[17] The protection of rights improves social utility by making people feel more secure, and security is "the most vital of all interests" and the one that "no human being can do without."[18]

As previously discussed, the vesting of individual rights leads directly to the threatened-rights-violation version of coercion. Having rights is only meaningful and only maximizes social utility to the extent that these rights are in fact protected. Utility is maximized not merely by telling individuals they possess rights but by protecting their possession of these rights. Utility maximization requires that if an individual makes a decision in order to avoid a rights violation, the decision is socially invalid and void. This is the only way to reaffirm for both the threatened individual and others the sanctity of the right. The protection of rights is necessary for individual security and security is necessary for individual happiness—utilitarianism's goal.

Posner takes pains both to distance his theory of wealth maximization from traditional utilitarianism and to explain why it provides a stronger grounding for vesting individual rights.[19] According to both Posner and standard economic theory, in the absence of transaction costs it would not matter in terms of the allocation of resources who was initially assigned different rights because the rights would be costlessly reallocated to whoever valued them most.[20] If, however, transaction costs exist, as they invariably do, then in order to achieve a wealth-maximizing outcome, rights must be initially vested in those who are likely to value them most.[21]

Posner's critical, and also perhaps uncontroversial, assumption is that individuals value rights to their own bodies and property more than do third parties. Posner explains that "[t]his is the economic reason for giving a worker the right to sell his labor and a woman the right to determine her sexual partners. If assigned randomly to strangers these rights would generally (not invariably) be repurchased by the worker and the woman respectively."[22] Thus, wealth maximization, like standard utilitarianism, vests rights in the individual.

As with utilitarianism, wealth maximization explains why decisions made in order to avoid rights violations are held to be invalid and nonbinding. If third parties were able to win goods or services by threatening to deprive others of their rights, they would be winning goods or services without having to pay what they are worth. Threats are inconsistent with a theory of wealth maximization because they take goods away from their highest-value user.

Utility maximization, either in its traditional form of happiness maximization or the economic form of wealth maximization, justifies both vesting rights in individuals and invalidating choices made in response to threatened rights violations. Moreover, these theories of maximization justify a traditional conception of coercion without relying on any substantive or controversial conception of human flourishing.

2. Kantian Justifications A second neutral justification for the threatened-rights-violation version of coercion is Kantian in nature. I use the term "Kantian" here to describe not only Kant's own maxims but those theories that ground themselves on certain foundational principles of how society should be organized and how individuals should behave. These theories do not rely upon, or suggest, any substantive conception of the good or meaningful individual human life. Instead, they derive rights from foundational principles of social organization. As with the utilitarian theories discussed above, acceptance of the threatened-rights-violation version of coercion follows directly from the vesting of individual rights.

In *Groundwork of the Metaphysic of Morals,* Kant sets forth his own universal moral laws derived a priori from pure reason.[23] Kant's categorical imperative commands: "Act only on that maxim through which you can at the same time will that it should become a universal law."[24] Kant's second moral principle, which he calls the practical imperative, demands that individuals must always treat themselves and others "never simply as a means but always at the same time as an end."[25]

The vesting of individual rights and the invalidation of choices made in response to threatened rights violations follow directly from both the practical and categorical imperatives. The notion that individuals are "ends in themselves"[26] argues in favor of vesting individuals with certain rights. Treating an individual as an end in herself requires respecting her rights, as well as her plans and projects. Allowing an individual to take something from another solely for her own pleasure while providing nothing in return is to treat the other solely as a means to the taker's happiness and not also as an end in herself.

The categorical imperative also justifies the vesting of rights in the individual and the invalidation of coerced choices. From Kant's examples of what could and could not qualify as a categorical imperative, it is clear that threatening another's life or property in order to get something that one wants could not be a categorical imperative. One could not will the universal maxim that everyone who desires something that another person owns may threaten to take her life or other possessions in order to get the thing that she desires. Such a universal maxim collapses on itself because no one could be said to own anything for others to covet if in fact everyone had a right to take by force whatever they wanted. Kant's imperatives, thereby, justify both the vesting of individual rights and the threatened-rights-violation version of coercion.

Ronald Dworkin presents a contemporary Kantian rationale for rights. Dworkin calls his foundational principle "the liberal conception of equality."[27] As with traditional Kantianism, Dworkin's principle of the right way to structure society is deliberately independent of any theory of the good way to lead individual lives. Dworkin's foundational postulate states:

> Government must treat those whom it governs with concern, that is, as human beings who are capable of suffering and frustration, and with respect, that is, as human beings who are capable of forming and acting on intelligent conceptions of how their lives should be lived. Government must not only treat people with concern and respect, but with equal concern and respect. It must not distribute goods or opportunities unequally on the ground that some citizens are entitled to more because they are worthy of more concern. It must not constrain liberty on the ground that one citizen's conception of the good life of one group is nobler or superior to another's.[28]

Dworkin's foundational postulate requires vesting particular rights in individuals to satisfy the postulate's demand that people be treated with concern and respect.[29] The postulate requires vesting the same rights in all individuals to satisfy its demand of equal concern and respect for individuals. Once rights are vested, it follows that threats to destroy them are impermissible and decisions made in response to such threats are nonbinding.

3. Conventionalist Justifications Conventionalism provides a third neutral justification for both the threatened-rights-violation and threatened-baseline-violation versions of coercion. Conventionalism argues against change and for retaining the status quo in order to maintain social stability and satisfy existing expectations. Conventionalism justifies the continued protection of individual rights for social reasons independent of any conception of human flourishing.

Probably the strongest conventionalist arguments have been made by Edmund Burke. Burke argued that sudden social change was dangerous and should be avoided. Necessary social change should be slow and cautious.[30] According to Burke, even small changes to the social structure can lead, through a domino effect, to the total destruction of the state, causing great psychological trauma for individuals.[31] Individuals gain a sense of belonging from their connection, through traditions and laws, to generations past and future. They structure their lives based on the expectation of the stability of social rules and institutions.[32] The status quo feels "natural" to people.[33]

Burke's conventionalism justifies the existence of certain individual rights and requires that choices made in response to threatened rights violations be void. Individuals are entitled to rights, such as bodily integrity and private property, because people are accustomed to having such rights. People believe that the rights belong to them by nature, and they structure their lives according to the expectation that these rights will be protected. Individuals would not make such investments in themselves or put such effort into acquiring possessions if they were not confident that the rewards of these efforts would be protected by the state.[34] In order for these rights people are accustomed to truly to be vested, violations of these rights, and decisions made in order to avoid violations of these rights, must be considered socially invalid and illegitimate.

Charles Fried argues that conventionalism better explains the substance of our individual rights than either utilitarianism or Kantianism.[35] According to Fried, conventionalism, rather than utilitarianism or Kantianism, gives individual rights their practical dimensions and force.

Fried criticizes utilitarians for underestimating the extent to which law is really about rights and not about the pursuit of social goals.[36] He criticizes Kantians for overestimating the extent to which they can describe and explain the law using philosophical principles.[37] Fried argues that while philosophical principles are useful as general guidelines for how the state should be organized, they do not answer the practical questions of what rights entail.

For example, philosophy may argue on behalf of protecting individuals from involuntary infringements of their person or property, it may argue on behalf of a private sphere that should be relatively free from state intervention, and it may argue in favor of a zone of personal privacy. Philosophy cannot, however, describe the specific shape of these rights. It cannot explain which activities fall under these general philosophical guidelines and which do not. Fried explains:

> Political philosophy can tell us that a just regime, a regime of liberty, is one in which persons have rights. . . . Philosophy may be able to tell us in a general way what some of these rights should be. . . . But it is preposterous to imagine that philosophy can tell us whether there should be a right to pri-

vacy in a public telephone booth or in a department store dressing room, or whether the imperative that property rights be respected includes the right of ancient lights or the use of percolating waters.[38]

Philosophy outlines the general structure, but law must embody a level of specificity and complexity that philosophy cannot impose.[39]

According to Fried, since the law cannot be based on philosophy it must be based on analogy and precedent. "Analogy and precedent are the stuff of the law because they are the only form of reasoning left to the law when general philosophical structures and deductive reasoning give out, overwhelmed by the mass of particular details."[40] It is convention, rather than philosophy, which defines the substance of individual rights.

Fried's conventionalism justifies and explains the rights-violation version of coercion in the same way Burke's did. Individuals are used to having rights to bodily integrity, property, and autonomy. Threats made to these rights, and decisions made in reaction to such threats, are invalid because a true vesting of rights requires that rights cannot be taken without the holders' consent.

The conventionalist justification for the threatened-baseline-violation version of coercion is similar. There are certain baseline conditions of well-being which, though they may not qualify as rights, are thought of as entitlements for those who possess them. Consider a case similar to the one involving the financial donor to the all-male school discussed above. An adult individual has always received a certain monthly allowance from a parent with no strings attached but also with no formal promise that the payments will continue indefinitely. Many people might come after a period of time to view the payments as a form of entitlement such that if the parent suddenly made the payments conditional upon the child marrying a particular person of the parent's choice, they would consider that choice to be coerced. Alternatively, consider an elderly man living alone in an apartment he has lived in for the past thirty years, paying essentially the same rent with increases matching the rate of inflation. His baseline condition of well-being is living in the apartment. If his landlord suddenly told him he must pay twice the amount of rent or move out, many people might consider the man's choice coerced.

If an individual has a reasonable expectation of stability in her baseline situation, then threats to that baseline look coercive. The threatened-baseline version of coercion relies, of course, on social agreement about individual entitlement to particular conditions. Since there is less social consensus about entitlement to baseline conditions than there is consensus about entitlement to rights, this version of coercion is less socially salient than the threatened-rights-violation version of coercion.

4. *Autonomy-Based Justifications* Arguments based on autonomy present a weakly perfectionist justification for the threatened-rights-violation version of coercion. The arguments are weakly perfectionist because they focus on the importance of individual self-determination for human flourishing while remaining silent about the particular ends toward which individuals should direct their lives.[41] As discussed in the introduction, an endorsement of the value of autonomy does not necessarily shift one from being liberal to being perfectionist. Liberals themselves are divided over whether autonomy may be adopted as a liberal value or whether its endorsement embodies too substantive a conception of the good to be compatible with liberalism's purported value neutrality.[42]

Many theorists argue that autonomy is fundamental to being human and is a fundamental human good. For example, Ernest Weinrib argues that the capacity for autonomy and the ability to act in accordance with the rule of reason distinguishes humans from animals.[43] Joel Feinberg argues autonomy is a fundamental good because it is a precondition to discovering one's other desires and values.[44]

Theories focusing on the value of autonomy tend to converge on two related conceptions of autonomy: the first involves the freedom of one's will from substitution by another person's will; the second involves the freedom of one's choice set from constraint. Cass Sunstein and Brian Barry offer conceptions of autonomy that require both types of freedom. According to Sunstein, "A citizen can be understood as autonomous insofar as she is able to choose among a set of reasonably good options and is reflective and deliberative about her choice."[45] According to Barry, "what is of central importance in human life is that people should make up their own minds about how to live and what to think and that they should be able to express their beliefs freely and act on their conclusions about the best way to live."[46]

Gerald Dworkin suggests two ways in which an endorsement of autonomy justifies acceptance of the rights-violation version of coercion. The first argument Dworkin presents is his own and focuses on the distinction between first- and second-order desires. The second argument he presents follows from Robert Nozick's analysis of metachoices.

According to Dworkin, the reason that choices made in response to threatened rights violations are a troubling violation of autonomy is because the agent's first-order preferences are incongruent with her second-order preferences. When faced with the choice "Your money or your life," the individual may affirmatively want to hand over her wallet. Her first-order preference is to do so. Dworkin argues we must look beyond first-order preferences in order to determine why acting to avoid a threatened rights violation infringes upon autonomy but acting for other reasons may not. We must look to second-order preferences. Second-order preferences reflect the conditions and motivations under which the individual would like to manifest her first-order preferences.[47] According to Dworkin, people normally do not mind acting if they believe they are improving their situation, but "[p]eople resent acting merely in order to retain a status quo against the interference of another agent (threats)."[48] Acting in order to maintain one's rights obviously does not improve the decision maker's position.

The second justification Dworkin presents for treating threats as an infringement on autonomy is based on Robert Nozick's concept of metachoices. Threats are different from other kinds of offers one might be presented with because rational agents would prefer not to be faced with a threat but they might choose to be presented with additional offers. Threats are a violation of autonomy while offers are not because the individual would prefer not to be presented with the threatening choice set at all—her metachoice would be not to be confronted with the choice. According to Dworkin, "we determine whether the agent is free by looking at the 'metachoices' that he would make."[49]

Dworkin explains that choices made in response to threatened rights violations are incompatible with an adequate protection of autonomy. Autonomy arguments, therefore, provide yet another, essentially neutral, justification for the vesting of rights and for invalidating choices made in response to threatened rights violations.[50]

II. Seductive Offers: A Nonstandard Version of Coercion

While feminists do, of course, challenge choices that are coerced according to the traditional model, feminists' distinct contribution to our thinking about power and inequality comes in their choice critiques that do not fit the standard coercion model. Most of the choices feminists challenge using the language of coercion are not coerced in the traditional sense.[51]

As described in chapter 2, feminists often use the language of coercion to challenge women's choices to commodify their sexuality, objectify their sexuality, and become full-time homemakers. These choices are generally not, however, made in response to threatened rights violations and are not coerced in the traditional sense.

For example, feminists criticize women's choices to become sex workers as not sufficiently free because the work provides many women's only or best means of financial support. The woman who becomes a prostitute in order to avoid starvation and homelessness, however, is not threatened with the loss of some specific good to which she has a right. The woman is not threatened with the loss of things she owns, but with the inability to continue to purchase things she needs. One might, of course, argue that the woman is being threatened with the deprivation of goods to which she has a social entitlement. However, society's failure to provide goods for its poorest members differs from a threat to take away that which a person already owns. Similarly, the woman who commodifies her sexuality because doing so will provide her with greater financial rewards than she can expect from other employment options is not responding to any threatened rights violation. She is not being forced into prostitution to protect her body or property from harm. Instead, she is making a choice to maximize her income that in some ways simply looks like a savvy career move.

Some feminists argue that women are coerced into objectifying themselves for men because of a fear of losing love, social acceptance, and recognition if they do not. While fearing loss of love or decline in social value because of a refusal to maximize one's value as an object is both real and painful, such fear does not constitute a threatened violation of any right the woman holds. Women have no right to a particular level of love and social attention, or any right for love and attention to remain constant throughout their lives.

Some feminists also argue that women are pressured to become full-time homemakers by the social message that good mothering is incompatible with serious work. However, the subliminal or direct messages many women receive telling them "Stay home with your children and people will think you're a good mommy" or "Devote your time to child care and housework and the family will be better off" do not involve threats to any rights the women hold. Women do not have a right to be thought of as good parents.

Although feminists use the strong language of coercion in justifying their challenges to these choices, these choices are not coerced according to the standard conception. Rather, they are made in response to choice sets that are hard to resist and which, some feminists believe, individuals should not be faced with. I call these choice sets "seductive offers." Seductive offers involve choice sets in which something about the nature of the two options being paired makes the choice seem coerced even though neither option threatens the individual's rights.

A. Defining Seductive Offers

The focus of seductive offers is not exclusively on the threat prong of the proposal, the "or else" in a "do X or else" proposal, as is the case in the traditional conceptions of coercion. Instead, the focus of seductive offers is on the interplay of the two prongs and on whether the contingent part of the proposal is a legitimate reason to do something that the agent would not otherwise do.

The term "seductive offer" typically and most intuitively describes offers of the form "do X and you will get Y." However, I am also using "seductive offer" to describe proposals that take the form of a threat, "do X or I will do Y to you," where Y does not involve a threatened rights violation. I am doing so for two reasons. First, most threats that do not involve rights violations can also be framed as seductive offers and vice versa. Consider the following examples: "Stay home with the kids or else people will think you're a bad mommy," as "Stay home with the kids and people will think you're a good mommy"; "Have sex with me or else I'll break up with you," as "Have sex with me and I'll continue to date you"; and "Have sex with me or else I will not give you that undeserved A," as "Have sex with me and I'll give you an undeserved A." Second, what is problematic and arguably coercive about the two kinds of proposals is similar. For both seductive offers and non-rights-violating threats, what makes the choice set coercive is something about how the two options interact with each other and whether one option, Y, is a reasonable basis for choosing the other option, X. In both cases, what is "coercive" about the proposal is not the prospect of either option taken by itself but the interplay of the two options. Certain choices should not be made for certain reasons, regardless of whether the options are paired against each other in the form of a threat or an offer.

Once we move away from coercion claims of the type "do X or I'll do Y to you," where either X or Y is something illegal or immoral and therefore never permissible for the offeror to do, and start looking at proposals in which both X and Y would, under different circumstances, be perfectly acceptable for the offeror to propose, it becomes much more difficult to explain what about the pairing of X and Y makes the choice seem oppressive. For example, "your money or your life" is clearly a coercive proposal because it is always immoral and illegal to propose to take another person's life without provocation. The proposal "have sex with me or you're fired" is a more difficult proposal, though there is pretty solid agreement these days that such a proposal imposes inappropriate pressure on a worker.[52] On their own, however, each part of this proposal set is acceptable. It is generally considered fine to ask someone to have sex with you and it is also generally nonproblematic for a supervisor to threaten to fire an underling, at least where the employee is an at-will employee. What makes the proposal oppressive in this case is something about how these two options interact with each other. The pairing of the options against each other makes the choice set problematic. It is this something about the interaction of the two independently unobjectionable options that is hard to pinpoint and that makes seductive offers considerably harder to define than the more standard coercive threats discussed in the last chapter.

Imagine a case in which A tells B, "If you do X, I'll do Y." In the seductive-offer scenario the focus is not on whether Y violates B's rights but on what X consists of and whether Y is considered an appropriate or inappropriate reason for doing it. There may be certain choices, such as X, that should not be made in order to get or avoid W, Y, or Z even if W, Y, and Z do not threaten B's rights. We seem to intuitively believe that there are intrinsically good and bad reasons for making certain decisions, and a proposal may seem coercive if it makes a choice tempting but for reasons that we feel should not be used to make that particular choice more appealing.

Margaret Jane Radin's discussion of choice incommensurability suggests what makes seductive offers seem coercive. Radin argues that there are certain human aspects and attributes that cannot be weighed against or exchanged with other goods and services without destroying the unique value of that thing.[53] In her view, babies and human sexuality are both incommensurable goods that cannot be traded for money or some other good without doing violence to our conception of what it means to be human.[54] Radin suggests not only that incommensurable goods cannot and should not be compared with or balanced against other goods and services, but that simply being presented with a choice set that attempts to do so does harm to the individual.[55] Just being presented with the choice to commodify an essential human attribute changes the individual in a harmful way by making her think about herself and her attributes as potentially fungible, exchangeable objects.

The theory of seductive offers is that certain goods or services simply should not be compared because one option cannot be a legitimate reason for performing or giving the other option. Merely being presented with the choice set and the trade-off possibility of the two options does harm to the individual by changing the way she thinks about the goods or attributes involved.

B. Examples of Seductive Offers

Consider the case of a male professor who tells a female student that if she has sex with him he will give her an A in a class in which she deserves a B. Assuming that the professor does not either explicitly or implicitly threaten to take away the student's deserved B if she refuses to have sex with him, then the professor's proposal is not coercive under either the rights-violation or baseline-violation version of coercion. The student does not have a right to an A. Since the professor's proposal can also be stated as "Have sex with me or I'll give you the B you earned," it is clear that the student's right to her fairly deserved grade is not being threatened. Similarly, the student's status quo level of well-being is not being threatened. If she does nothing, the student receives the B she deserves. Yet, even so, many people would intuitively find the professor's proposal coercive and oppressive.[56] We may think there are a range of legitimate reasons to choose to have sex with someone, but that getting an undeserved A is not among them.

Consider the similar case discussed previously, of the boy who tells his girl-friend that unless she has sex with him, he will break up with her. As with the case of grades for sex, this proposal does not threaten to violate any right that the girl is entitled to nor does it threaten to diminish her status quo level of well-being if that is understood to be that she will continue being involved in a relationship with her boyfriend only so long as both parties are satisfied with the terms of their involvement. Those who intuitively find such a proposal coercive probably do so because they think the decision about whether to have sex with someone should not be made out of fear of losing one's relationship with that person. To make someone decide whether to have sex based on such a fear imposes inappropriate pressure on the decision maker.

Compare the previous choice set, which at least some people would probably find coercive, with the following one, which probably many fewer people would find so. A and B have been dating for two years, at which point B says to A, "Come to my family's house for Thanksgiving or I will break up with you." This situation parallels the dating scenario in that the proposal does not threaten to violate any right that A holds, nor does it threaten to worsen her status quo level of well-being if such is taken to be, as it was above, that she is involved in a relationship only so long as both parties are happy with its terms. This proposal, though parallel to the one presented above, seems distinctly less oppressive.

One might argue that the difference between the proposals and what makes the "have sex or break up" proposal seem more coercive than the "home for the holidays" proposal is that A's decision of whether or not to go to her partner's relatives' house for Thanksgiving gives her partner important and relevant information about their relationship. One might initially think that what distinguishes the two proposals is their relative information value for the proposer. In fact, though, the information value to the proposer is no less significant in the "have sex or break up" proposal. The boy making such a proposal certainly learns important information about the nature of his relationship by seeing whether his girlfriend will have sex with him. The difference in how the two choice sets are perceived is due not to how legitimate or useful the knowledge rendered is but to the nature of the act proposed, the nature of the thing promised, and their interrelationship.

Consider these further examples. First, imagine a professor tells a student that if he washes the professor's car the student will receive an A that he does not deserve. If he refuses to wash the professor's car he will receive the B he earned in the class. Some people might think the choice to wash a professor's car in exchange for a higher grade is coercive even though neither the student's rights nor his baseline condition of well-being is threatened. The student does not deserve an A in this case so his rights are not being violated. If he decides not to wash the professor's car, he will be in the same situation he was in before the professor made his proposal: receiving the grade he earned. Therefore, the proposal does not threaten to worsen his status quo level of well-being. As in the cases presented above, those who view this choice as coercive probably do so because they think the decision of whether to wash someone else's car should not be made in order to gain an A in a class. There are a whole range of legitimate reasons why one might choose to wash someone else's car: for money, as a favor, in exchange for some comparable service. But improving one's class grade is not a reasonable basis upon which to decide whether to wash another person's car.

Alternatively, one might see this case and the one involving sex for an A as dissimilar in important respects. The proposal in this case may seem less coercive than the sex for an A proposal. Since the two proposals do not differ with respect to whether they confront the chooser with a threatened rights violation or a status quo violation, any difference between the two in terms of their perceived coerciveness must be attributed to differences in the things being requested by the proposer. One might think that the service of washing a person's car is just a commodity which, like money, can be offered and exchanged for an A. By offering the student the option of exchanging car-washing services for an unearned A, the professor may be breaching some ethical obligation that he has to grade fairly, but the student is simply choosing whether to participate in a market transaction similar to those made every time he enters a supermarket and exchanges money for food. According to this interpretation, the car washing in exchange for an A is no more coercive than the multitude of commodity transactions that we engage in every day.

If an A is viewed as a commodity that can be bought or exchanged, like car washing, while sex is viewed as a noncommodity that cannot be bought or exchanged, then the proposal exchanging car washing for an A may be seen as a noncoercive commodity exchange while the proposal exchanging sex for an A may be seen as coercive because it forces an individual to try to balance and compare incommensurable goods. If, however, an A is viewed as incommensurable with anything other than a particular quality of work, then proposals to exchange either car washing or sex for an A are likely to both be viewed as coercive.

III. Feminists' Criticism of Seductive Offers

Many of the choices feminists challenge using the language of coercion are not coerced in the traditional sense but are instead made in response to seductive offers. The choices are problematic because they are the product of choice sets that feminists think women should not have to face. Consider again feminists' criticism of women's choices to commodify their sexuality, objectify their sexuality, and become full-time homemakers.

Feminists who criticize women's decisions to commodify their sexuality by arguing that the choice is "coercive" or oppressive probably feel that women should not be presented with the choice to commodify themselves and certainly should not be presented with a choice set in which sexual commodification promises their greatest financial rewards. Women should not be forced to think of their sexuality as a potential commodity by being presented with the option of selling it for large financial gain. Sexual commodification is degrading, but financial reward is difficult to resist. The choice set is both appealing and dangerous; and therein lies its oppressiveness.

Women's choices to sexually objectify themselves probably look problematic and pressured to some feminists because they feel women should not be presented with the choice of whether to turn themselves into decorative gift objects for men's gratification in order to achieve their highest possible social status. Women should not be asked to balance and weigh their agency and personhood against promises for social love and respect. The choice set is not coercive in the traditional sense, but it puts inappropriate and harmful pressure on the individual.

Similarly, feminists' arguments that women are pressured into becoming full-time homemakers are not criticisms of choices made in response to coercive threats but of choices made in response to seductive offers. To the extent this choice set looks problematic to feminists, it is because there is something about the nature and importance of parenthood, and probably also about paid employment, such that women should not face an either/or choice between the two.

IV. Nonperfectionist Rationales Cannot Justify
This Expanded Version of Coercion

Both the concept of seductive offers and feminists' criticism of choices made in response to seductive offers are distinctly nonneutral and perfectionist. Challenging a choice because it arose from a seductive offer involves an openly perfectionist judgment about the kinds of choices individuals should and should not make as well as the appropriate considerations to be taken into account for particular choices. What is problematic about seductive offers cannot be explained by resort to the same neutral rationales offered to explain why coerced choices are illegitimate.

A. Kantian Justifications Fail

Although one can enlist a Kantian justification for the rights-violation version of coercion, the same is not true for the seductive-offers version. First, seductive offers do not threaten to treat individuals solely as means and not also as ends. A seductive offer such as "have sex with me and I'll give you an undeserved A" does not treat the decision maker as a means solely for the proposer's ends. The agent has a choice of whether or not to engage in the exchange of sex for an A and presumably would not engage in it if she did not feel that she was getting something more valuable out of the exchange than she was giving. The agent might be making a choice to exchange her body for a grade which she would not have made if the professor had not given her such a proposal. And she might prefer overall that she did not have the choice to make in the first place. However, the choice does not treat the woman solely as a means but also as an end. She has the option to either remain in her present situation or to use her body as a means to an end that she desires.

Second, seductive offers do not violate the categorical imperative. One could will that people can be presented with any choice sets or exchange options that do not contain threats to protected rights. The only reason one could identify for not wanting individuals to be subject to any and all possible choice sets is if one believed that certain options should not be balanced against each other and certain goods or services should not be bartered for others. This belief, however, cannot be justified by resort to either the categorical imperative or the practical imperative but only by resort to perfectionist beliefs about what goods and services are incommensurable or incapable of commodification and barter.

B. Utilitarian Justifications Fail

Similarly, the seductive-offers rationale of coercion cannot be justified by resort to utilitarianism. It is difficult to argue that overall social happiness is maximized by not allowing individuals to present others with seductive offers. Even if we assume that an individual presented with a seductive offer is happier before she is presented with the choice set than she is afterward, it does not follow that overall happiness is increased by not allowing individuals to present others with seductive proposals. Assume the woman who is presented with the proposal "prostitute yourself and get lots of money" is happier before she is presented with the proposal than she is afterward. Assume also that if the woman chooses to prostitute herself, it is because she values the money more than she values the absence of a commodified sexual exchange. It is certainly plausible that the increase in overall happiness that people get from being able to make whatever proposals they want to other people—so long as these proposals do not involve threatened rights violations —outweighs the level of utility that would result if people were restricted from presenting others with seductive offers.

C. Conventionalist Justifications Fail

The lack of any shared agreement about what choice sets constitute seductive offers suggests the impossibility of restricting seductive offers based on convention. Unlike the fairly long-standing social expectations that all persons in America are entitled to rights to bodily integrity and to personal property free from attacks and threats of attacks, there is no such similar widespread understanding about individuals being entitled to not be presented with certain option sets and to not have to make certain decisions. There is not widespread agreement, probably even among feminists, that certain choice sets should be off-limits. For example, many feminists would probably criticize as "coercive" the boyfriend's proposal to his girlfriend that she have sex with him or he would break up with her. They might argue that a girl should not be forced to decide between her bodily integrity and her relationship. However, there is no general social agreement that girls should not be faced with this particular choice or that, more generally, woman should never be forced to make decisions relating to their sexuality to which negative consequences attach.

D. Autonomy-Based Justifications Are Inadequate

Similarly, a concern for autonomy does not justify a restriction on seductive offers. In situations involving traditional coercion, lack of autonomy is signaled by the loss of a particular option. Before being presented with the threat "Do X, or I'll kill you," the individual was capable of choosing from a range of options A through X. The coercive threat deprives her of choices A through W and leaves her with only two choices, X or death. Seductive offers differ in one important respect from coercive threats: they do not involve the loss of any particular end-state option. An individual presented with the seductive offer "Do X, and I'll give you Y" retains the whole option set of A through X that she had prior to the proposal.

For example, it is difficult to argue that presenting a woman with the choice to either stay home with her children or go to work infringes on her autonomy even if both choices bring with them different social and economic consequences. Even phrased as the seductive offer "Stay home with the kids and everyone will think you're a good mommy," it is clear that this choice set does not diminish the woman's choices in any way from what they were previously but only presents her with one additional option and its likely consequences. Similarly, the female student presented with her professor's proposal to "have sex with me and I'll give you an undeserved A" does not suffer any loss of autonomy. She retains all the options she had previously with respect to her academic and personal life and now simply has one additional option. Prior to the seductive offer she could only get an A in the course by improving her test grades; now she has another possible way to achieve her goal of better grades. If anything, her autonomy seems enhanced by the proposal.

What the individual does lose by being presented with a seductive offer is not a particular option, but the ability to live without a particular option set. She loses the ability not to be tempted by this particular choice set and hence loses the option of remaining in her pre-seductive-offer state. What makes the imposition of a tempting choice set problematic is less about individual autonomy than it is about perfectionism.

The only way that presenting individuals with additional choices can be harmful to autonomy is if one infuses the conception of autonomy with a perfectionist vision of human flourishing. One might argue that certain choices by their mere presence harm the individual. They are harmful, though, because of the nature of the temptation they present to the individual, not because of any formal constraint they place on her choice set. Some seductive offers encourage a less valuable vision of autonomy for a woman by encouraging her to think about herself and her attributes in a particularly harmful way. Such a perfectionist version of autonomy, of course, is incompatible with the nonperfectionist version used to justify standard coercion claims.

A closer look at Gerald Dworkin's theories about why threats involve problematic autonomy violations does suggest a possible rationale for finding seductive offers problematic without resort to perfectionism. But this rationale does not in fact seem to be a plausible account of feminists' criticism of the seductive offers discussed here.

If, as Dworkin's second theory suggests, what determines whether a particular choice constitutes a problematic autonomy infringement is the individual's preference never to have been faced with the choice at all, then autonomy violations become purely subject-dependent. This subjectivity may be less problematic with respect to threats because of the assumption that people uniformly prefer not to be faced with threats to their person and property. This subjectivity constraint is a bigger problem with respect to seductive offers. Women would probably disagree about whether they prefer to be presented with seductive choice sets. Some eighteen-year-old female students might prefer to have the option to have sex with their professors as a way to raise their grades while others would hate being encouraged to think of themselves and their sexuality as objects for exchange and would strongly prefer never to have the option. Similarly, some women would probably prefer having the option to have sex for money while others would find the option repugnant to their self-conceptions.[57]

This highly subjective conception of autonomy cannot, however, explain feminists' criticism of certain seductive offers which applies regardless of the personal preferences of the recipient of the offer. For example, for feminists critical of sexual commodification, choice sets offering women their highest economic rewards for sex work are problematic for all women, not simply those who would subjectively prefer not to be faced with the choice.

Conclusion

The goal of this chapter has been twofold: to explain traditional liberal conceptions of coercion and to show that most feminist choice critiques that are framed in terms of coercion are grounded instead on the perfectionist conception of seductive offers. The chapter has argued that many choices feminists criticize and challenge using the language of coercion are not coerced. Instead the choices are the product of seductive offers. What is problematic about these choices can only be understood by resorting to the perfectionist idea that individuals should not be presented with certain choices and trade-offs because they should not be encouraged to think about their characteristics and attributes in particular ways.

The next chapter analyzes feminists' arguments that certain choices women make are illegitimate or suspect because they are the product of sexist socialization. I argue that these criticisms, too, rely ultimately on a perfectionist conception of human flourishing.

5   Socialization Critiques

The second major way in which feminists challenge women's choices is by arguing that they are the product of a restrictive and sexist socialization. The socialization renders the choices suspect. Choices made under fair and just conditions are legitimate and accepted while choices made under unjust conditions are distorted, illegitimate, and subject to challenge.

Socialization-based criticisms sound neutral because they focus on the conditions under which choices are made rather than the choices themselves. Choices are criticized not because of their substance or quality, but because they are the product of unfair social conditions. However, despite their neutral ring, socialization-based choice critiques rely upon perfectionist conceptions of human flourishing to inform their conceptions of both appropriate conditions and outcomes.

This chapter first analyzes the socialization argument that most closely resembles the traditional coercion critiques discussed in the last chapter. This "method of socialization" choice critique challenges the legitimacy of choices that are the product of socializing environments characterized by threatened and actual rights violations. It is the method of socialization by which preferences are formed that renders the resulting choices subject to question. This section points out the hazy line between coercion and socialization yet argues that despite the similarity, the choice critique based on method of socialization is not neutral and cannot be justified by the same neutral arguments that justified the traditional conception of coercion. The remainder of the chapter considers more general socialization-based justifications for challenging women's choices and argues that they too are motivated by perfectionist conceptions of how individuals should be encouraged to live their lives.

I. Method-of-Socialization-Based Choice Critiques

This narrow socialization-based choice critique argues that certain choices women make are illegitimate because women's preferences are formed through a socialization process consisting of threatened or actual rights violations. The method of socialization renders individuals' resulting preference orderings illegitimate and their decisions open to challenge.

The argument consists of two claims. First, threatened rights violations constitute an illegitimate background condition under which to develop one's preferences. Second, preferences formed under these conditions are likely to be different from the preferences that would have developed under fair or just conditions.

For example, feminists often focus on the fact that many women who become prostitutes have suffered sexual abuse as children and argue that this socialization process undermines the legitimacy of these women's choices.[1] The argument, most notably made by Catharine MacKinnon, is that women have been socialized under conditions of systemic sexual violence to think of themselves as, and to become, sexual objects and sexual commodities for men's enjoyment. According to MacKinnon, "more than one-third of all girls experience sex, perhaps are sexually initiated, under conditions that even this society recognizes are forced or at least unequal. Perhaps they learn this process of sexualized dominance as sex. Top-down relations feel sexual."[2] In this view, women's preferences and choices are suspect because they are the product of a violent socializing environment.[3]

Robin West makes a similar argument. West argues that women's choices should be viewed critically and challenged because they are the product of dangerous and threatening environments. West argues that violence permeates many women's lives and defines their sense of self. According to West, "women's lives are dangerous, and it is the acquisitive and potentially violent nature of male sexuality which is the cause of the danger. A fully justified fear of acquisitive and violent male sexuality consequently permeates many women's—perhaps all women's—sexual and emotional self-definition."[4] As a result of this violent socialization, many women do not behave like the self-interest maximizers liberal society expects. "The inescapable fact," West explains, "is that much of the misery women endure is fully 'consensual.'"[5] West argues that feminists must not merely accept women's choices at face value as reflecting true and legitimate desires, but must challenge the context in which women's preferences are formed and choices are made.[6]

The method-of-socialization argument sounds neutral because its focus is on the conditions under which women form preferences rather than on the substance of the preferences adopted. As West argues, "If we are going to address the causes of our misery, then we must attack the context, not the choices themselves, for signs of bondage."[7] The idea behind the argument is that it is worse for a woman to think of herself as a sex pet because she was sexually molested as a child, bombarded with pornography, and threatened with various other forms of sexual violation than it is to think of herself as a sex pet because she had a subscription to *Glamour Magazine* from the time she was ten or simply because she had always been voyeuristically sexualized by adults in the way that pretty little girls in our society frequently are.[8] Choices are challenged only because of the conditions of which they are a product.

Method-of-socialization-based choice critiques and coercion critiques lie on a continuum, and the distinction between the two is often hazy. Imagine a fourteen-year-old girl who is routinely presented by the boys she dates with the implicit choice to have sex with them or to face an uncertain consequence ranging from violence to anger to mild disappointment. The girl does not want to have sex but feels that she must in order to avoid some negative consequence. The girl's choice might be considered coerced in a quasi-traditional sense. Although the girl is not making her decision in response to a direct threat of sexual violence, she is making her decision in response to a probabilistic threat of violence; the girl may know that there is a 15 percent chance that any boy she tries to refuse sex to will rape her. Imagine the same girl two years later. She has been out on many more dates and faced many more demands for sex. On some occasions she declined and was raped; on some occasions she declined and was verbally harassed; on some occasions she declined and nothing happened. On some occasions she agreed to have sex. By the time the girl is sixteen she no longer wants to decline sex and face the uncertainty of the boy's "or else." Instead, she conceives of herself and has come to understand herself as a successful sex object whose purpose and goal is to have sex with the boys who desire to have sex with her. She affirmatively wants to have sex with the boys who date her. She knows this is what they want from her, and she has come to understand and value herself as one who is sexually attractive and available to men. The girl's choice to have sex looks much less coerced and looks more like a product of socialization at sixteen than at fourteen.

The question as one moves from coercion choice critiques to socialization-based choice critiques is whether the girl's choice is any more problematic at fourteen, when she decides to have sex because she fears the consequences of refusal, than it is at sixteen, when she wants to have sex because prior experiences of sexual violation and sexual threats have taught her that she is valued primarily for sex. The method-of-socialization choice critique argues that the sixteen-year-old's desire to have sex is open to challenge and criticism precisely because her preferences were formed in reaction to a series of threatened rights violations. Just as the fourteen-year-old's decision to have sex in order to avoid a threatened rights violation is considered illegitimate, so too is the sixteen-year-old's desire to have sex considered illegitimate where such preference was cultivated by a series of threatened rights violations.

Despite the similarity between method-of-socialization critiques and coercion critiques, however, there is no neutral justification for challenging all choices arising out of a socialization environment characterized by threatened rights violations. The claim that all choices made by women socialized in a context characterized by threatened rights violations are illegitimate and invalid cannot be justified by appealing to the same neutral rationales that explained the social illegitimacy of coerced choices.

Utilitarianism justified the threatened-rights violation version of coercion because it seemed sensible and uncontroversial to hold that all people are happiest when they possess rights to their own body and personal property. In order to make these rights meaningful, individuals cannot be threatened or violated without punishment to the abuser. In order to preserve the meaningfulness of individuals' vested rights, any decisions that they make in order to avoid violations of their rights are considered invalid and nonbinding. The same logic does not render illegitimate choices resulting from a more diffusely violent process. Once an individual is acting according to what she understands to be her most favored preference, regardless of where her preference ordering came from, it is unlikely that her happiness, and that of the others socialized in the same way, will be maximized by treating all her life choices as illegitimate.[9] It is impossible to imagine that social utility could be maximized by challenging the validity of all life choices made by individuals socialized in a context characterized by threatened rights violations. These individuals whose decisions are challenged may be "better off" according to some measure of welfare, but they certainly will not be happier by having their preferred choices delegitimized.

Challenging such socialized choices cannot be well grounded on Kantian rationales either. One could not will as a universal maxim that all of the life choices made by individuals who have been socialized in a context characterized by rights violations are invalid and nonbinding. Since one would rarely know whether another person's preference orderings, and hence her life choices, were the result of a socialization characterized by threatened rights violations, everyone would have to treat everyone else's choices as though they did result from such socialization and hence were invalid. As a result, one could not be held to a stated goal or promise, nor would one find social support and protection for one's chosen life paths. Society would devolve into a morass of mistrust and failed cooperation. Everyone's life choices and projects would be treated by others as though they were illegitimate and invalid.

No individual could will that her chosen life paths and projects not be respected and protected by those on whom she must rely and with whom she must interact. Furthermore, denying the legitimacy of all individuals' choices and stated preferences clearly violates the practical imperative by refusing to treat individuals as ends in themselves, at least according to how they have defined their own ends.

Moreover, there is no justification based on convention for challenging and criticizing all choices made by individuals who have been socialized through a process involving threatened rights violations. All individuals, regardless of how they have come to hold the goals, preferences, and priorities that they do, expect that their life choices and projects will be granted the same social respect and protection that is granted to anyone else's choices.

Certainly, too, a respect for autonomy does not support challenging all choices made by individuals who have been socialized through threatened rights violations. The threatened-rights-violation method of socialization obviously affects an individual's preferences, as does any form of socialization, but the individual's particular choices still reflect her own self-determination and will. Furthermore, the rights-violation method of socialization does not actually constrict the individual's choice set but only affects what it is she desires. At the time the individual is making a choice, she has a full range of options; her preferences, however, have been shaped by her socialization.

Even Dworkin's theory about threatened rights violations being a problematic incursion on autonomy because they violate people's second-order preferences—those regarding the conditions under which they want to make choices—does not extend to the rights-violation method of socialization. What distinguishes threat-based socialization from direct threats is that in the latter case one's decision is made in response to and as a direct condition of the threat while in the former case decisions are made under conditions that may themselves be entirely unthreatening and unproblematic. An individual may not object at all to the conditions under which she makes a particular choice even though her more general socializing conditions are characterized by rights violations. Hence, it is unlikely that one could challenge on autonomy grounds the legitimacy of all choices made by individuals socialized through threatened rights violations.

In fact, it is unclear what rationale would ground a consistent ideological critique of all choices made by individuals whose preference orderings have been formed in an environment characterized by threatened rights violations. It is difficult to explain why all choices, not simply those responding to direct threats, should be rendered illegitimate because of the background conditions under which an individual came to hold her preferences.

In practice, feminists do not challenge all choices made by individuals so-cialized in a particular environment but only those that seem responsive in a harmful way to the rights-violating aspects of their socialization. It is this selectivity that most clearly reveals the perfectionism underlying the method of socialization-based choice critiques.

For example, while feminists criticize and challenge the choices of women who have been victims of childhood sexual abuse to become prostitutes, they do not challenge these women's choices to become doctors or lawyers.[10] Probably the first choice seems more a reaction to the rights-violation aspect of their socialization than does the second. However, feminists also do not seem to criticize or challenge sexual-abuse victims' choices to become sex-ual-assault counselors instead of prostitutes. In this case, both choices seem responsive to the rights violations the victims endured, but they are respon-sive in different directions.

Kathryn Abrams addresses the difficult balance for feminists between rec-ognizing the extent to which women are constructed by the sexual violence which pervades their lives, and trying to give women credit for actions which Abrams views as exhibiting their own "agency." Abrams suggests that to the extent women's choices are the product of their violent environments they are subject to criticism and challenge, but to the extent they express true agency they are deserving of respect. Abrams explains that agency can exist under conditions of coercion but it is a partial agency "confined by social and structural constraints that complicate the path to action, and . . . impeded by women's own internalization of society's derogation."[11] According to Abrams, "[t]he battered woman who seeks counseling, demands a safer en-vironment for her children or risks separation abuse by trying to distance herself from her spouse . . . exercises political agency."[12]

Of course, in practice the difference between choices reflecting one's agency and those reflecting one's violent socialization is virtually impossible to discern. Although Abrams praises women's decisions to leave battering relationships as an exercise of autonomy and would probably criticize women's decisions to stay in such relationships as an example of "ideologically determined" be-havior,[13] in fact both of these choices reflect women's different reactions to socialization conditions involving prior rights violations. Praising one deci-sion as reflecting agency and criticizing the other decision as reflecting the influence of one's violent socialization simply masks the real reason Abrams and other feminists distinguish between choices. What is really at issue is a substantive judgment that, in such circumstances, the decision to leave is bet-ter than the decision to stay.

Feminists might argue they prefer the decision to leave over the decision to stay only because they want the woman to avoid the future rights violations that are likely to occur if she stays in the relationship. Feminists might argue that their selective critique is based not on a perfectionist conception of human flourishing but on an essentially liberal concern for the woman's safety both at the present time and in the future. While this argument might explain feminists' selective choice critiques in situations in which one choice does bear a high probability of future rights violation, it cannot explain their selective critiques in situations in which none of the woman's choices involve highly probable future rights violations.

Imagine, for example, a young woman who was molested repeatedly during her childhood by an uncle. In her adolescence and early adulthood she has chosen to have sex with many men as a way to feel loved and valued. She has no sense of self-worth except as a sexual object and it is only while acting as such that she ever feels confident and sure of herself. The woman has recently, however, decided to press criminal charges against the uncle who molested her as a child and to confront other family members about the blind eye they turned toward the abuse she suffered.

Many feminists would probably want to challenge the woman's choice to become a sex pet for men but would applaud her choice to confront her molester and her family. Yet, both decisions arose out of the same method of socialization and neither involves a particularly high likelihood of future rights violation.[14] The first choice may seem more in keeping with the woman's violent socialization and the second choice may seem more like a reaction to it, but both are products of her socialization.

Feminists' selective-choice critique does not reflect a consistent concern about the legitimacy of choices resulting from a socialization characterized by threatened rights violations. All decisions made by women in such situations are affected by the violent socialization. The selective criticism shows a substantive preference for certain choices over others and reveals the perfectionism actually informing feminists' socialization-based choice critiques.

Feminists might also argue that they selectively criticize only those choices that seem directly motivated by specific prior rights violations. They might argue that some decisions, like the decision to leave an abusive relationship, grow out of the neutral or good aspects of women's socialization, while other decisions, like the decision to stay in an abusive relationship, reflect the rights-violating aspects of their socialization. Feminists might argue that they criticize only those choices that are the product of violent and degrading socializing messages.

This attempt to distinguish the choices one wants to criticize from those one wants to validate based on the socializing force behind the choice is problematic. While it is probably the case that different choices are affected to varying degrees by different socializing forces, it seems unlikely that theorists can actually identify the primary motivating conditions behind different choices. And it is too simplistic to think that particular socializing forces always direct choices in the same direction. Violent socializing conditions will not always produce masochistic or self-degrading choices but will sometimes produce just the opposite. Consider the battered woman who leaves the abusive relationship, prosecutes her abuser in court, and becomes a counselor for other women. Certainly her actions are motivated by her history of abuse, but feminists would not want to criticize these choices just because of the causal link.

Additionally, it is likely that many choices are motivated by different and even contradictory socializing conditions, making identification of the primary or responsible one impossible. A woman's decision to leave her abusive husband after several years may be both a reaction to the abuse which she could no longer tolerate as well as a response to her participation in a feminist reading group. Arguing that the choice is primarily a response to the non-rights-violating book club rather than the rights-violating beatings seems untestable, and motivated solely by a desire to validate that particular choice.

If feminists want to challenge the validity of women's choices because they are the product of socialization characterized by threatened or actual rights violations, they must challenge the validity of all the choices women make under such socializing conditions. As discussed previously, such a blanket criticism is difficult to justify on any grounds. To pick and choose some decisions to criticize and others to praise when all arise out of the same troubled method of socialization is to make perfectionist judgments about good and bad life choices rather than neutral procedural claims about the appropriate background conditions for choice.

II. Authentic Choices

Most generally, socialization-based choice critiques argue that women are socialized to hold preferences that are distortions of their true underlying preferences. The idea is that women possess authentic desires but their current choices do not reflect them. Women have been socialized to think that they want to do and be things that they really do not want to do and be. Their choices are "inauthentic."

The claim is that authentic choices and preferences are those made and held under procedurally correct conditions while inauthentic choices and preferences arise out of procedurally flawed conditions. Inauthentic choices are illegitimate and subject to challenge and criticism.

Procedurally flawed conditions may be those characterized by rights violations,[15] those teaching gender hierarchy,[16] or those discouraging reflective decision making.[17] The ostensible target of socialization arguments is a type of socialization, not particular choices.

For example, Rita Freedman criticizes the social pressures that encourage girls and women to sexually objectify themselves. She argues that girls choose to turn themselves into decorative sex objects for men in response to society's message that their social value depends on their success at doing so.[18] She suggests that because the choices seem causally linked to these socializing forces and messages, the choices are not true or authentic. Reva Landau and Susan Okin make similar socialization-based arguments in their criticism of women's choices to become full-time homemakers. Both argue that women's choices to become full-time homemakers cannot be considered true and authentic when they are made in a society that encourages girls and pressures women to play such a role.[19]

As with the method-of-socialization arguments, these more general socialization arguments ultimately rely on perfectionist judgments about what kinds of choices are compatible and incompatible with a good human life. All social contexts shape individual preferences and encourage certain choices. Both the decision of what constitutes an uncorrupted socializing condition and of when such a condition has been reached rely on a substantive conception of how individuals should live their lives.

First, consider the argument made implicitly or explicitly by many feminists that only choices made under conditions of gender equality can be considered true choices. Conditions of social gender equality can only be seen as promoting authentic choices if individuals' authentic choices are already assumed to be consistent with the socializing pressures of a gender-egalitarian society. If women authentically crave to be subordinate to men and men authentically crave to dominate women, then socialization in a society promoting gender equality will distort rather than reinforce authentic preferences. For a fundamentalist Christian, authentic choices are those that arise out of a socializing context that encourages firmly divided gender roles. A social context encouraging the full participation of both sexes in all aspects of society would be seen as distorting authentic preferences.[20]

Since there is no neutral, or nonsocializing, social context within which individuals can make their choices, claims that certain social contexts distort authentic choices while others protect or encourage authentic choices rest initially on a substantive conception of authentic choices. Since no one, of course, knows what individuals' authentic choices would be, or if such choices could ever exist, the concept of authenticity is simply a proxy for the kinds of choices the theorist thinks individuals should make.

Second, determining when the theoretically pure condition has been achieved in practice also relies on a judgment about appropriate outcomes. Since there is no objective point at which one knows the theoretically ideal conditions have been achieved, one can assume they exist only when the choices people make match those one would expect them to make under such conditions.

Consider again the claim that authentic choices arise out of egalitarian environments. Imagine a hypothetical feminist who argues that women's choices should be considered fully legitimate and authentic as long as they are made under conditions of gender equality. How can she determine when equal conditions have been achieved except by reference to the choices she thinks would arise under such conditions?

Some people, for example, will tell the feminist that equality presently exists in our society. Women and men have approximately equal formal access to education and to almost all public-sphere activities. They share equally in the right to participate in the life and governance of their civic communities. According to this view, women's choices arising under current social conditions should be viewed as authentic and be free from challenge. The feminist, however, may argue that current conditions cannot be fully equal because women and men continue to live very different types of lives; women become primary caregivers for their families while men become primary providers. Such dramatically different choices could not be the result of truly equal socializing conditions.

The feminist may argue that an egalitarian society requires not only equal formal access to education and careers but also certain structural features— easily available contraceptives and abortions, maternity leave policies, and publicly funded child care centers—in order to ensure that women are able to take advantage of their formally equal rights. However, if these changes are achieved and women and men continue to live very different kinds of lives, our feminist might go even farther.

She might argue that an egalitarian society requires not just the formal rights and social structures described above but also that girls and boys be raised in families that treat them similarly and that encourage them toward the same socially valuable pursuits without regard to sex. She might argue that equality requires that women no longer be sexualized and valued socially in accordance with their sexual attractiveness and availability to men. And she might argue that social equality requires the curtailment of sexual violence against girls and women.

The point is, there is no clear stopping point for our feminist. There is no natural or objective place at which point one must say social equality has been achieved.[21] Innumerable modifications and alterations are possible to our laws, education system, and popular culture to make social conditions seem somehow more equal for women and men.[22] In a sense, one knows equality has been achieved only when individuals are making the choices one would expect them to make under such conditions. Until outcomes match expectations there is no reason to decide equal conditions exist.

Consider the similar claim that authentic choices are those that are made under conditions of reflection, consideration, and thoughtful challenge from others who are familiar with one's experiences and desires. As in the prior case, deciding when the appropriate pure and nondistorting procedure has been achieved ultimately rests on judgments about what authentic preferences look like, which again rests on perfectionist judgments about what kinds of life choices and preferences are in keeping with a good human life and what kinds are not.

Determining when the pure procedure has been reached in this case is really an issue of when to stop the questioning. At what point has the decision maker been challenged enough and been self-reflective enough so that her decision should be accepted as authentic?

Imagine a young woman who marries her male professor, conceives of herself primarily as a sexual object, and gives up her own career aspirations in order to support his. At her first consciousness-raising group she says she is happy with her life and her choices. Other women in the group ask whether she feels a sense of loss or a lack of fulfillment. She says she does not. At her second consciousness-raising meeting the woman is again asked whether she regrets not pursuing her academic potential, whether she craves validation for her own accomplishments, and whether she thinks that she gave up her own career aspirations simply because society convinced her that she was not as worthy of care and respect because she is a woman. The woman answers again that she is happy with her decision to give up her academic aspirations and does not believe she is suffering from false consciousness by believing that her husband's mind is more worthy of cultivation than her own.

Why does the consciousness-raising questioning not stop there? Why would the proper procedure for making authentic decisions not exist until the fiftieth or one-hundredth consciousness-raising session when the woman finally says that she now recognizes how she was raised to believe that she would never contribute as much to the world as a scholar as she would as a mother and that she now regrets her acceptance of such sex stereotypes?

Furthermore, why should the procedure be considered complete at this stage? Why should the questioning not continue further to a point where the woman might very well come to believe that her husband really is a remarkable man who, all sexual stereotyping aside, was a worthy investment of her time and attention?

There is no implicitly logical point at which to decide that the context of procedural purity has been achieved.[23] One can only decide that such a procedure exists or does not yet exist when one compares the choices that are being made with those one thinks are authentic and hence would be made under conditions of procedural purity. In other words, the questioning only stops when the person gives the "perfect" answer.

Conclusion

Socialization-based arguments, like coercion arguments, sound neutral because they focus on the conditions under which choices are made rather than the choices themselves. As this chapter argues, however, this distinction is illusory. Feminists' conception of what socializing conditions are fair and just is based on a substantive conception of how people should live. No social context is neutral. The conditions favored by feminists are those designed to encourage particular kinds of lives and activities. Furthermore, feminists' selective criticism of particular choices, when all of a person's choices are the product of the same socializing context, belies feminists' claims of outcome neutrality. At root, feminists are concerned with whether women are making good or bad life choices regardless of the socializing context of which they are a product.

6 Equality Arguments

As the previous chapter argued, feminists often explicitly or implicitly suggest that women's choices are not "real" or legitimate because they are made under conditions of gender inequality. The chapter considered this argument in the context of a larger discussion of the effects of women's socialization on the "authenticity" of their choices. This chapter analyzes and tries to explain a narrower equality argument: unless women and men are faced with the same life choices, neither group's choices can be considered wholly legitimate.

Equality arguments straddle both coercion and socialization arguments and can be framed as a version of either. Equality arguments can be framed as a version of a coercion argument by claiming that women's decisions seem "coerced" or forced because women make their choices from a different set of options than men face.[1] Alternatively, equality arguments can be framed, as they were in the last chapter, as a version of a socialization argument by claiming that women come to desire and choose the life paths they do because of the distinctly gendered options they are presented with.

The equality arguments feminists make suggest that creating equal choice sets requires more than giving nominally similar choices to similarly situated women and men. Choice-set equality requires that women and men face the same choices having the same meaning and the same degree of attainability.

For example, both Catharine MacKinnon and Susan Hunter suggest that women's choices to commodify their sexuality are not true choices. They view these choices with skepticism because women make them without as many or as good alternatives available to them as are available to men. Both argue that the choice to commodify one's sexuality should not be accorded the sanctity normally given to individual choices in a liberal society because women typically make this choice from such a restricted set of options. According to MacKinnon, "Women's precluded options in societies that discriminate on the basis of sex, including in employment, are fundamental to the prostitution context. If prostitution is a free choice," she asks, "why are the women with the fewest choices the ones most often found doing it."[2] Hunter asks us to "explore the meaning of 'choice' in prostitution by looking at the sphere of choices available to or withheld from all women. . . . Right now for all women choices are severely limited by the poor, second class status dealt to us."[3]

Susan Okin and Joan Williams challenge women's choices to become homemakers on the same grounds. Because women are presented with a very different set of life choices and options than are men, women's choices cannot be treated as reflective of their true desires. Okin suggests that women's and men's career and family choices must be viewed with skepticism because of the different options presented to both. "Socialization and the culture in general place more emphasis on marriage for girls than for boys. . . . This fact, together with their expectation of being the parent primarily responsible for children, clearly affects women's decisions about the extent and field of education and training they will pursue, and their degree of purposiveness about career."[4] Williams encourages feminists to challenge rather than ratify and accept women's choices. "Feminists need to arm women to resist the argument that women's economic marginalization is the product of their own choice. Challenging this argument should be easy, since, in fact, in our deeply gendered system men and women face very different choices indeed. Whereas women, in order to be ideal workers, have to chose not to fulfill their 'family responsibilities,' men do not."[5]

While feminists who argue that women and men should face similar life choices do not specify the precise parameters and requirements of the equality they demand, they are clearly seeking a more substantive vision of equality than the formal equality of opportunity that presently exists. Feminist equality arguments suggest a conception of equal choice sets requiring that women and men face not only the same formal choices but also the same real choices —choices having the same meaning and the same availability for both sexes.

In this section, I work through several thought experiments in order to discern what it would mean for two people or two groups of people to truly face the same set of options. What does it mean for individuals to be presented with the same choices having the same meaning and the same degree of attainability? In the next section, I ask whether such a conception of equality is justifiable.

On the most basic level, choice sets are thought to be equal if they are the same size, that is, if they contain the same number of choices. Even on this seemingly simple level, however, comparisons of choice sets are complicated. Size comparisons of sets only make sense if there exists a common metric for the elements of the different sets such that one set contains all the items of the other set plus something more. Sets cannot be compared as larger or smaller if they contain different items. A straight ordinal counting of the substantively different items in two sets does not translate into any kind of meaningful set comparison. For example, set X can only be compared with set Y if X contains A,B,C and Y contains A,B,C + D,E. The set composed of A,B cannot be compared, however, to the set composed of C,D,E. The fact that the second set contains "more" elements is meaningless as a stand-alone criterion. It may make sense, for example, to say that the choice set containing mop, clean dishes, do laundry, is larger than the set containing mop, clean dishes. It makes no sense, however, to say that the set containing mop, clean dishes, do laundry, is larger than the set containing mop, practice law.[6] There is no way to compare these different items or the sets they compose.

Consider a concrete example of this general principle of choice-set incommensurability. Compare the choice sets available to girls in single-sex and co-ed schools. In a co-ed school a girl could choose to be on the math team with boys, to be a cheerleader for boys, to be homecoming queen, to be in school government, or to perform a range of other roles and activities with other girls and boys. In a single-sex school a girl could choose to be on the math team with girls, to be on the soccer team, to be part of the popular crowd, to participate in school government, or to perform a range of other roles and activities with other girls. These choice sets cannot be compared as larger or smaller than each other because there is no way to compare the elements in each set.

In addition to rendering size comparisons impossible, the existence of different elements in different choice sets renders even seemingly similar choices within the sets substantively different. Choice-set context changes the intrinsic nature of choices, rendering nonidentical choice sets incommensurable. Each element that is added to a choice set changes the meaning of the elements already present in the set. For example, a particular choice is different when it is the only member of a choice set and when it is a part of a group of choices. The choice set composed of A,B is not identical to the choice set containing A alone joined with the choice set containing B alone. When dealing with choice sets, A,B does not equal A + B. It is likely that the choice set A,B has changed what it means to choose A simply by offering A within the context of also offering B. The choice set combining A and B becomes A′,B′. Similarly, A is substantively different when combined with B than when combined with C.

Consider two concrete examples of how choice-set context affects the intrinsic nature of particular choices. First, consider the difference between Amishness chosen from a set of different life choices and Amishness chosen from a set where it is one's only option. Assume that one is presented with the choice set consisting of the full range of cosmopolitan options: "A,B,C, . . . Z." Included in this set, of course, is the choice to be Amish. Cosmopolitanism, however, does not simply offer an individual the same choice to be Amish that is offered to members of an Old Amish community and then add to that a whole range of other choices: to be Muslim or Jewish, to become a doctor or a fashion model, to endorse evolution or creationism. The very ideology of cosmopolitan choice means that the Amishness presented in the cosmopolitan choice set is dramatically different from the Amishness presented in the Amish-only set.

The goal of cosmopolitanism is self-expression and self-realization. Cosmopolitanism presents individuals with a wide range of options; they choose the one that will bring them the most pleasure and gratification. Choosing to be Amish from a choice set presenting no alternatives has nothing to do with self-expression, self-realization, or personal gratification. It is about duty and obligation. One may at some point come to believe that Amishness best fosters one's self-realization but this is not the reason Amishness is chosen. The very considerations of personal fulfillment and self-gratification that are necessarily part of the Amishness chosen from the cosmopolitan choice set are anathema to the Amishness assumed as one's duty and responsibility.[7] One cannot be Amish in the same wholly unquestioning way when one chooses Amishness under cosmopolitanism as when one is raised to be Amish in an Old Amish community and given no other options.

In essence, this was the legal claim of parents in *Wisconsin v. Yoder*,[8] in which the Supreme Court held that members of the Old Order Amish Community in Wisconsin were not bound by the state's mandatory school attendance laws for children up to the age of sixteen. Amish parents argued that mandatory schooling for their children past the eighth grade would endanger both their community survival and their children's salvation.[9] The parents in *Yoder* viewed the values and choices presented by the public schools as in direct conflict with the values of Amishness. Cosmopolitanism did include Amishness as one option among many but effectively eliminated the option to be Amish in the way the *Yoder* parents wanted their children to be Amish, unquestioningly and as a matter of duty, not choice.[10] The Amish parents objected to sending their children to public high schools in Wisconsin because the range of options presented there would change and undermine the meaning of being Amish as they understood it.[11]

Second, compare again the choice sets available to girls in co-ed and single-sex schools. It is not simply the case that girls' schools deprive girls of a whole range of sex-kitten options. Instead, all the choices of the two sets differ. Nominally similar options mean dramatically different things in the two contexts. For example, what it means for a girl to do school government or cheerleading in a co-ed school is completely different from what it means for a girl to do these things in a single-sex school. The girl who becomes class president in an all-girls school will not have the same experience as the girl who becomes class president in a co-ed school; she will be denied the opportunity to lead boys. Being a leader of girls is substantively different from being a leader of boys as well as girls. Similarly, cheerleading in a single-sex school is a substantively different experience from cheerleading in a co-ed school. A cheerleader in an all-girls school cheers for girls. She is deprived of the opportunity to cheer for boys as well as the opportunity to be part of a particular social crowd of male athletes and female cheerleaders.

The substantive changes in the choice to be class president or a member of the math team rest not wholly or necessarily on the actual presence or absence of boys from the school. It is possible to imagine two different girls' schools, one in which girls are presented with a wide range of sex-kitten options (suppose the school was designed as the sister school to a boys' school with which it has social events and for which the girls cheerlead), and a second one in which girls are not presented with sex-kitten options within the school (imagine the school's mission is to train future professionals). Being either class president or on the math team in the first school would differ significantly from filling one of these roles in the second school. The presence of sex-kitten options makes school government or math team participation intrinsically more butch and less feminine in the first school than the second. In the first school if "everyone knows" that school government is uncool because the sex-kitten options are more appealing, then in fact school government is uncool. Likewise, school government is cool in the second school because "everyone knows" it is a position of power and prestige. Furthermore, being class president in the first school means constantly refusing to retreat into any number of easy sex-kitten options while also having to recognize and probably pay some service to this range of options that many members of one's class do choose. Being class president in the second school does not involve the knowledge that one could always retreat back to the safety of sex-kitten status, nor does it require homage to this range of choices.

In addition to changing the intrinsic meaning of choices, choice-set context also changes the likelihood that a particular option will be chosen and acted upon. Choice sets look different when particular choices are more appealing in one choice set than they are in the other.

Most simply, as a person's choice set expands to include more appealing choices, the probability that she will choose the options that were previously available to her decreases. Particular options become less likely to be selected simply because the chooser is presented with more desirable options. The probability of attaining a particular option may also change because choices are more available or realizable in some contexts than in others. Finally, the probability of an option occurring may change as a result of changes in the preference ordering of the chooser: how desirable a choice is to the chooser may change for reasons internal to the chooser. I refer to these changes in attainability as (1) changes in straight probability; (2) changes in choice availability; and (3) changes in chooser preferences. Only the first type of probability changes do not render choice sets incommensurable.

Changes in straight probability mean that as one's choice set expands the probability that one will continue to select the same option diminishes because the larger choice set increases the likelihood that a more preferred option has become part of the choice set. The chooser's preference ordering is the same in both sets, and the likelihood that she can achieve each choice is the same for both sets. All that changes is the number of options present. This increase in options diminishes the probability that the option chosen in the smaller set will also be chosen in the larger set.

Consider a simple example. I am presented with an original choice set of vanilla and strawberry ice cream. I am ambivalent about vanilla ice cream and do not care much for strawberry. So, given this choice set, I have a 90 percent probability of choosing vanilla and a 10 percent probability of choosing strawberry. On my preference hierarchy of ice cream flavors, chocolate far exceeds both vanilla and strawberry. Suppose I am presented with a new choice set containing vanilla, strawberry, and chocolate ice cream. The probability of my choosing chocolate ice cream is 90 percent while the probability of my choosing vanilla or strawberry drops to 9 percent and 1 percent respectively simply in reaction to the inclusion in the choice set of an option I prefer.

Consider another example that is more relevant for feminists. A woman is initially faced with the career choice of secretary, nurse, or teacher. She has a one-third probability of choosing each option. The woman's choice set is then expanded to include the options of business executive, doctor, or professor. If the woman prefers any or all of these options to any of the ones presented in the prior choice set, then the probability of occurrence of the original choice-set options will decrease.

Changes in choice occurrence probabilities of this sort do not render choice sets incommensurable. The choices in both sets are equally available and feasible for the chooser, and they are equally appealing to the chooser both in absolute terms and in terms of their rank order on her preference hierarchy. The larger choice set simply provides a better opportunity for the chooser's underlying preferences to be realized. The two sets are commensurable because the nominally similar choices substantively and practically mean the same thing in both sets.

The two other kinds of choice probability changes—those due to changes in the availability of the choice and those due to changes in the chooser's desire for the choice—do render choice sets incommensurable. For example, a choice which exists in two choice sets may be much more available and free of external constraints in one set than the other. Comparing the size of sets in which the probability of choice occurrence differs for this reason is impossible. The sets look too different and mean different things to the chooser even though they contain substantively similar choices.

Imagine that vendor A offers me the choice of vanilla or chocolate ice cream while vendor B offers me the choice of thirty-one flavors. It may be that chocolate ice cream is actually more available to me from vendor A than from vendor B. Vendor A, who specializes in chocolate or vanilla ice cream, may keep more in stock than does vendor B, who must keep in stock a much larger array of flavors. Vendor B may, therefore, sell out of chocolate ice cream more frequently than vendor A, making the probability that I will actually get chocolate ice cream from vendor B lower than it is from vendor A. Comparing my flavor sets between the vendors is not possible if I do not really have the same chance to have chocolate ice cream from the two vendors.

Similarly, Amishness is a less achievable choice in the cosmopolitan set than it is in the Amishness-only set even if one desires Amishness the same amount in both contexts. Cosmopolitanism imposes higher costs on the realization of Amishness than does the Amish-only choice set due to the transition costs of entry into the Amish community that are not present for the individual who is Amish by duty. Amishness looks like a different choice in the two sets not simply because it means different things intrinsically but because the degree to which the choice is really available to the chooser differs between the sets. This difference between the two sets in the possibility of realizing the choice renders the sets incomparable.

Probably the clearest example of the way that choice-set context changes the availability of particular choices and renders the choice sets incommensurable is the comparison of nominally similar choices in girls' schools and co-ed schools. As with the Amishness example, the choice to be class president in a co-ed school differs from the same choice in an all-girls school not only because the choices intrinsically mean different things, but because the choice for a girl to be class president in the all-girls school seems like a much more real, achievable option, than does this same choice in a co-ed school. A girl in a co-ed school may be less likely to become class president than a girl in a single-sex school due to sexism, the tracking of girls away from student government, and the refusal of at least some boys to vote for a girl. It would not make sense to say that the co-ed school choice set of class president, math team captain, cheerleader is larger than the girls' school choice set of class president and math team captain, even if these choices meant intrinsically the same things. The availability of the options are so different in the two sets as to make set comparisons meaningless. The choice sets no longer look the same when the possibility of achieving the same options are far less likely or possible in one set than in the other.

It is this intuition of incommensurability which drives some feminists to the logically inconsistent, though revealing position of preferring a cosmopolitan choice set over an Amish one and a single-sex school choice set over a co-ed school one. One can only prefer cosmopolitanism over Amishness by claiming that the range of options presented by cosmopolitanism is larger and by ignoring the low probability of occurrence of most of the choices. In contrast, one can only claim the girls' school choice set is larger and hence preferable to the co-ed choice set by focusing on the higher probability that girls will actually choose and obtain certain favored options in single-sex schools and by discounting the value of a whole range of options available to girls in co-ed schools that are not present in girls' schools. In the first instance feminists determine the "larger" choice set and ignore the probability of particular choice occurrence, while in the second instance feminists only determine which is the "larger" choice set by finding that certain favored options are more likely to occur in girls' schools than in co-ed schools.

The probability of occurrence of the same option in different choice sets also changes due to changes in how much the chooser likes the option, both in absolute terms and in terms of its placement in her preference hierarchy. Again, probability-of-occurrence changes of this sort render choice sets incommensurable. Even choice sets containing substantively similar options look too different to be comparable when the same choices mean new and different things for the chooser depending upon their context.

For example, assume I originally have a preference for chocolate ice cream over all vanilla and vanilla-based ice cream flavors. When presented with chocolate, vanilla, and chocolate chip ice cream, I always prefer chocolate. It is possible, though, that I may actually like chocolate less when I am presented with the thirty-one flavors of Baskin-Robbins instead of my original three. It is not just that having thirty-one flavors better reflects my true preference ordering so that I am now able to choose fudge brownie instead of choosing chocolate because all along fudge brownie was at the very top of my preference ordering. Instead, I actually like chocolate ice cream less, both in absolute terms and in terms of my preference ordering, when it is presented alongside thirty other flavors. Whereas in the first context a chocolate ice cream cone would give me fifteen minutes of intense pleasure, in the second context it gives me only five. In the first context I really do prefer chocolate to all vanilla-based flavors, while in the second context I actually want cookies and cream instead of chocolate.

A similar change in chooser preferences may take place with respect to Amishness when it is presented as one's only option and when it is presented as one choice among many. One may actually want to be Amish less when Amishness is presented in conjunction with lots of other choices than when it is presented alone. As above, it is not just that the larger choice set better reflects the chooser's stable and pre-existing preferences but that her preferences change, at least in absolute terms if not also in their rank order. As with chocolate ice cream, Amishness is simply less appealing, interesting, and exciting when presented alongside a multitude of choices than it was when presented alone. Amishness is not just outranked in the larger choice set by more preferred options; it actually seems more nerdy and unappealing than it did when presented alone. The Amishness choice, even if substantively identical in the two sets, means different things to the chooser and this difference in meaning renders the sets incommensurable.

Again, the most relevant example of changes in chooser preferences involves the choice sets presented to girls in co-ed and single-sex schools. A girl may be much less likely to become class president in a co-ed school than in a single-sex school not only because of differences in option availability but also because of changes in how much the girl desires such a position in the two contexts. A girl may actually want to be class president more when she is not presented with a full range of sex-kitten options than when such options are available to her. It is not simply the case that the larger choice set better reflects the girl's preferences, but that the choice sets change her preferences. In the all-girls school a girl may prefer to be class president over being a cheerleader. In the co-ed school where the girl faces a much more diverse range of sex-kitten options—cheerleader, homecoming queen, girlfriend to a popular boy in school—the cheerleading option actually becomes much more attractive, so much so that she prefers being a cheerleader to being class president. It is meaningless to say that the co-ed choice set of class president, math team captain, girlfriend to a popular boy is larger than the girls' school choice set of class president, math team captain. The choice to be class president is so much less appealing to the girl in the co-ed school than it is to the girl in the single-sex school that it is no longer the same choice.

The distinction between substantive changes in particular choices and changes in chooser preferences for particular choices in different sets is blurry. Particularly if one considers the substance of a choice to include the social meaning of the choice and the chooser's internal understanding of the choice, then, necessarily, any time a choice becomes less attractive to the chooser, the substantive meaning of that choice has changed as well. For example, the fact that a girl thinks being on the math team is geeky when she is presented with a range of sex-kitten options but not when such options are absent is both because she takes a more boy-oriented viewpoint on the world when confronted with the sex-kitten options and because within this viewpoint the math team is substantively different: it is geeky. Preference changes cause substantive changes in the meaning of a choice just as substantive changes in choices affect a chooser's preferences.

An awareness of the difference in how available certain choices are and how they are perceived in different choice contexts is present in the literature advocating single-sex education. Many people advocating single-sex education for girls stress the fact that in girls-only schools, girls are more likely to participate in academic and school leadership activities and less likely to devote themselves to increasing their value as sex kittens. Commentators recognize that certain choices become both more attainable and more appealing for girls in girls-only schools than in co-ed schools.[12]

Many factors bear consideration when determining whether choice sets are equal in the substantive way feminists seem to desire. As the last section suggests, truly equal choice sets are difficult to conceptualize and impossible to actualize. Even were this not the case, however, it is also surprisingly difficult to justify why women and men should face equal choices sets.

Most often, equality arguments are premised on a liberal anti-discrimination principle: similarly situated people should be treated alike. Women and men are similar in their aptitudes and abilities and should, therefore, face the same set of options. If women and men do not face the same set of options, the cause must be impermissible status-based discrimination: treating similarly situated people differently because of an irrelevant characteristic such as sex.

The problem with the anti-discrimination argument is that sometimes women and men are not alike or similarly situated and sometimes sex is relevant to the options one faces. Women and men do differ in some important respects that may bear on how appealing or attainable certain choices are for each gender. Diverging choice sets may result not from status-based discrimination but from significant and salient gender-based differences.

It is difficult to justify why women and men should face the same options in cases in which gender has a material effect on how each gender relates to and performs a particular activity. For example, much has been written in support of girls and boys having equal athletic choices in high school and college athletics.[13] Less has been written advocating equality of choice sets at the level of professional athletics.[14] However, the difficulty raised by sex-based equality claims, as well as the need to articulate a justification for such claims, is clearer when thinking about the need for women and men to have equal choices regarding professional athletic careers. I use the example of equal choices with respect to professional athletics to point out the significant theoretical problems posed by arguing for choice equality between the sexes as a general principle.

Consider the argument that women and men should face the same set of options when deciding whether to play professional basketball or to pursue some other nonathletic career. Under this argument, Rebecca Lobo and Grant Hill, for example, as outstanding female and male basketball players, should face the same choice about pursuing a professional basketball career.

The claim that Lobo's choice set should look like Hill's cannot rely on a straight liberal anti-discrimination principle. Sex obviously is relevant to basketball: Lobo may be as talented a player as Hill but she is not as "good" a player as Hill in the most basic sense, because she would lose to him if they played a game of one-on-one. Similarly, it is likely that a team of professional women basketball players would be rather evenly matched by a team of good (but nonvarsity) male college players.[15]

Instead, the recognition of sex-based differences in basketball playing justifies the initial division of women and men into different fields of competition. Just as we do not think it is fair to have 150-pound men box against 300-pound men, we think it is not fair to make women compete directly with men in basketball. In the first case we think that weight is a relevant characteristic for group distinction while in the second case we think that sex is.

However, the fact that sex is a relevant characteristic to basketball playing, perhaps justifying different leagues for women and men, does not explain why Lobo's basketball options should be the same as Hill's. The best lightweight boxers do not get the same recognition and rewards as the best heavyweight boxers, nor do average male players get the same recognition as great male players. But, the equality argument requires not that Lobo have the same choice set as the average male players that she may be equivalent to—this would be a sex-is-irrelevant claim—but that Lobo have the same choice set as that of the most talented male players.

The anti-discrimination argument with respect to choice sets where sex is clearly relevant to the activities involved is more complicated and problematic than that made in cases where the irrelevance of sex is the basis for the anti-discrimination claim. In cases where sex is relevant, the anti-discrimination claim seems really to be a diversity claim. The argument is that women's basketball is so different from men's basketball so as to be essentially a different game. If women's basketball is not appreciated as much as men's basketball, it must be because women are generally devalued by our society. This diversity-based anti-discrimination argument raises more problems than it answers, however. First, to the extent that women's sports are significantly different than the corresponding versions that men play, there is increased likelihood and plausibility that the reason women's sports are less popular is because people prefer the men's version of the game for legitimate, non-status-based reasons. Second, if equality in women's and men's athletic choices is grounded in a diversity argument, then the strength of the equality argument weakens the more similar the women's and men's versions of a sport become. The argument for equal choices with respect to sports such as swimming or track and field—where it is hard to argue that women's version of the sport is substantially different from men's version of the sport and yet where the best women athletes cannot compete with the best male athletes— is greatly undermined. For these reasons, the anti-discrimination claim seems to be an insufficient grounding for an equality-of-choice-set argument in cases where sex is indeed relevant to the activity at issue.

One might argue Lobo's choices should match Hill's because, despite the difference in play, the inequality still reflects impermissible status-based discrimination against women. One may believe that the reason the market does not offer Lobo the same possible rewards that it offers Hill is because the market reflects sexist assumptions about the inappropriateness and inadequacy of women playing sports. Men just do not want to watch and cheer women's athletic pursuits for reasons independent of the quality and character of their play.

While there may be some truth to the discrimination argument, it is difficult to justify equal choices based solely on a hypothesis of insidious discrimination when a legitimate basis for women's and men's different choices is just as likely.[16] Because women and men really are different in their basketball abilities, these differences may legitimately affect the choices each is presented with. It is entirely plausible, for example, that at least some of the reason the market offers Lobo less is not because people value women less than men or think that women should not be athletes, but because sports fans prefer the game of men's basketball over women's basketball. It may be that the reason that Lobo does not have the same basketball options as Hill is because fans really prefer watching Hill play over watching Lobo play. He can dunk and she cannot, he can run faster than she can, and he can shoot from farther outside. Fans simply prefer watching Hill play because they prefer watching his talents and skills over watching Lobo's.

An argument for equal choices in this case must rely not merely on a recognition of the relevance of sex for basketball ability but also on a belief in the importance of social recognition and reward for the highest athletic achievement of both sexes. The argument is that women deserve the athletic options that men possess not because women will exercise those options in the same ways, or because they are similarly situated with respect to the options, but because the options are similarly important for the flourishing of both women and men.[17] In other words, the argument that women and men, despite their real and material differences in certain regards, should face equal choice sets is necessarily perfectionist.

Given the difficulty of justifying equal choices for women and men based on a liberal anti-discrimination principle alone, it is not surprising that feminists' real commitment to equality is pragmatic, not pure. Feminists' concern is not, in fact, with achieving or justifying a monstrously complicated conception of perfect equality, but with achieving a far more pragmatic and perfectionist assurance that women will have equal chances with men to achieve certain particularly important goals and accomplishments.

Feminists making equality arguments are not concerned with ensuring that every choice women and men face is the same, but with ensuring that women, like men, face certain choices that are particularly important for human flourishing. As was the case with feminists' socialization-based arguments, feminists' particularistic rather than systemic concern with achieving equality of certain choices reveals the perfectionism underlying their equality arguments.

Consider a hypothetical equality claim dealing with women's and men's relation to pregnancy. Imagine that in the next century technology is created by which fertilized embryos can exist and grow outside of a woman's womb. A purely ideological equality argument would require that women only use the artificial out-of-body wombs to bear children and never physically give birth to a child. Giving women and men the same choice sets with respect to having a child requires that they be similarly connected, or disconnected, to the actual birthing process.

It seems unlikely that any feminists arguing for equal choices would advocate a ban on women bearing children. Equality as a neutral principle does not drive the argument. Pregnancy and childbirth, though they may have social disadvantages attached to them, are unlikely to be viewed by many feminists as either incompatible with or required for a good human life.

Feminists like Okin, MacKinnon, Hunter, and Williams argue that women and men should face the same career opportunities. They do not spend time arguing that women and men should face the same choices regarding childbirth, hairstyles, or the social acceptability of wearing earrings. The choices they are concerned with are those to be lawyers, politicians, or primary parents. Feminists pick their battles based on the importance of the choices to the quality of individuals' lives. Feminists focus on women and men having the same range of public- and private-sphere opportunities available to them because such parity is critical to women's self-development and determination.

Not only are feminists concerned with equality of some types of choices but not others, they typically also have some conception about what these equal choices should look like. If feminists were truly concerned only with equality, they would be agnostic about what choices actually look like as long as women and men were presented with the same ones. This does not appear to be the case.

MacKinnon and Hunter, for example, focus on ensuring that women are presented with the same range of career opportunities that men are presented with. The equality envisioned is one in which women's choices come to look more like men's currently look than vice versa. MacKinnon and Hunter do not argue that men's choice to commodify their sexuality should come to look like women's but instead they argue that women's career opportunities should look more like men's.[18]

Okin, too, has a vision of what the equal choices women and men face should look like. According to Okin, women and men should face the same social encouragement and pressure to be both paid workers and primary parents.[19] Women and men should face choices that differ from the traditionally female one of domestic caregiver and from the traditionally male one of financial provider. Women and men should both face choices that encourage dual public- and private-sphere participation. Okin has a clear preference about what the equal choice set looks like. Okin is not neutral as to the set of choices both women and men should be presented with. She is advocating equal choices of a particular form, and it seems the form of the choices is more important that the fact of equality.

Conclusion

This chapter has pointed out the theoretical difficulty of conceptualizing and justifying truly equal choice sets between women and men in order to reinforce my argument that equality as a neutral principle is not what feminists are after. Feminists who criticize women's choices because they are made under conditions of gender inequality are not advocating equality for equality's sake. Instead, they are advocating equality because of what equality means for women in certain circumstances. Feminists' selective use of equality arguments combined with their substantive conception of what the desired equal choices should look like shows that feminists are concerned ultimately with ensuring that women have certain valuable opportunities available to them, not with ensuring that women and men face all the same options. At root, perfectionism, not egalitarianism, drives their arguments.

7 Vulnerability-Based Choice Critiques

A final type of argument feminists use to challenge and criticize women's choices focuses not on the conditions under which women make their choices but on the probable consequences of their choices. Vulnerability-based arguments criticize women's choices on the grounds that the choices will make them vulnerable to some future harm. The arguments may initially sound neutral because they do not criticize choices based on the substance or meaning of the choices themselves but focus instead on the likely consequences of the choices. This appearance of neutrality is, however, largely illusory. While there is a neutral-vulnerability argument, this is not the form feminist vulnerability arguments take. Feminist vulnerability arguments are distinctly perfectionist.

Vulnerability arguments are neutral when they focus entirely on inadequacies in the decision maker's thought processes. Neutral-vulnerability arguments focus on the rational inconsistencies or factual inaccuracies that mar the decision maker's thought processes. The vulnerability to be avoided is not the risk of a particular outcome but the risk of regret likely to result from a poorly made choice. For example, one might challenge a woman's choice to become a homemaker or sex worker by arguing that she does not understand what her choice really entails (for example, how hard it will be to re-enter the labor force after leaving it, or how violent sex work really is) or that the woman is discounting future risks (she believes she and her husband will never divorce; she believes she will be able to choose safe men). The woman is making choices that entail risks she might not want to accept if she knew their true magnitude. As a result, the woman is likely to regret her choices.

This vulnerability-based argument is neutral about the kinds of life choices women make and the kinds of risk they accept. As long as women make informed choices and accept risks knowingly, it does not matter what choices they make or what risks they accept. The argument respects existing preferences and individual autonomy. It simply points out an individual's logical failings in order to ensure that her true preferences are reflected in her choices.

Neutral vulnerability arguments are of limited usefulness, however, because the grounds for criticism disappear as soon as one educates the decision maker. Imagine a feminist who criticizes a woman's choice to prostitute herself as irrational and ill-informed. If the woman, after hearing all the relevant information regarding the future risks and payoffs of her choice, continues to want to prostitute herself, the feminist is left with no further recourse but to stop criticizing her choice or to adopt an openly perfectionist stance. The perfectionist stance argues that the choice is a mistake because its likely consequences are incompatible with human flourishing, regardless of the woman's informed judgment to the contrary.

This more openly perfectionist vulnerability argument challenges choices not because of the process by which they are made but because of the substantive outcomes to which they are likely to lead. Not surprisingly, feminists' vulnerability arguments take this perfectionist form. Feminists criticize choices they think expose women to excessive risk of certain kinds of harms regardless of whether these choices are made by clueless women who do not know what their choices entail or by knowledgeable women aware of the risks involved. Ultimately, feminists are concerned not with women's thought processes and background information but with their actual choices and what these choices mean for women's lives.

For example, Catharine MacKinnon and Nancy Erbe are both critical of women's decisions to become sex workers because the choice makes women highly vulnerable to physical violence. According to MacKinnon, "Women in prostitution are subject to near total domination."[1] Erbe agrees: "Regardless of how women are procured for prostitution, pimps control prostitutes after they enter prostitution."[2] MacKinnon and Erbe do not, however, restrict their criticism to the choices of girls or naive women who enter prostitution with no idea of the risks they are accepting. Their arguments may be strongest and most persuasive with respect to this population, but their criticism is not limited to these particular women. MacKinnon and Erbe criticize women's choices to become prostitutes because the choice is dangerous and degrading regardless of whether it is made with full information or in total ignorance of the risks involved.

Feminists also challenge choices that make women vulnerable not to liberal rights violations, as is the case with prostitution, but to outcomes that are harmful only according to a perfectionist vision of human flourishing. Feminists challenge women's choices to become sex objects and homemakers on the grounds that these choices make women vulnerable to a loss of self-respect. Upon examination, however, it appears that feminists are not concerned with ensuring that women possess a simple baseline level of self-respect but are instead concerned with the nature of women's self-respect and how their self-respect compares to that of the men in their lives. Feminists' concerns go beyond a liberal acceptance of self-respect as a primary good and reflect instead a substantive conception of human flourishing.

For example, Rita Freedman criticizes women's choices to sexually objectify themselves on the grounds that doing so makes women vulnerable to a significant loss of self-esteem in the future. As women's sex-object value declines, they are left with little self-respect and little sense of self-value.[3]

On its face, this argument, like the last relating to physical safety, seeks to avoid the loss of some primary good—self-respect.[4] It is likely, however, that Freedman is concerned not simply with ensuring women possess self-respect but with encouraging women to possess particular kinds of self-respect. If Freedman and other feminists were motivated only by concern over the drop in women's self-respect accompanying their decline in value as sex objects, they would lose their ground for challenging sexual objectification if society suddenly began valuing women as objects at the same level over the course of their lives. It is difficult to believe that if the world were to change such that women were valued as sexual objects at the same level throughout their lives—either because society overcomes its obsession with youthful appearance, or because cosmetic surgery enables women to maintain the same appearance all their lives—that feminists would stop objecting to women's choices to self-objectify. Indeed, feminists might be even more likely to challenge women's decisions to objectify themselves in a society where such women would never be forced to develop a deeper sense of self.

It seems likely that Freedman's and other feminists' opposition to women's choices to self-objectify relies on perfectionist judgments about better and worse bases for self-respect. It is better to have self-respect based on confidence in one's innate and developed abilities and capacities than to have self-respect based on the value that others place on one's aesthetic being. The first kind of self-respect promotes human flourishing while the second kind does not. Freedman, in fact, is quite clear about the perfectionism underlying her opposition to self-objectification. "Objectification changes body image and erodes self-esteem. To be objectified means to be seen as a thing that exists for the viewer. As object rather than subject, a woman suffers a kind of 'psychic annihilation.' As object, her existence depends on the observer who can either bring her to life by recognizing her or snuff her out by ignoring her."[5] Self-respect as an object, it seems, is not valuable self-respect.

Margaret Baldwin and Susan Okin make a similar psychic vulnerability argument with respect to women's decisions to become full-time homemakers. Again, while the criticism at first seems based on the danger of a loss of self-respect, what appears really to be at stake is the kind and level of women's self-respect. Baldwin argues that full-time homemakers become psychologically and emotionally vulnerable as a result of their economic dependence on another individual. According to Baldwin, "Decades of research, as well as the voices of women in consciousness-raising, have documented the depression, disintegration of self, and passivity that so often overwhelm women engaged in full-time housework, until leaving the home becomes a nearly insurmountable challenge."[6] Similarly, Okin argues that "[t]he psychological effects on an adult of economic dependence can be great."[7]

These arguments are not merely about women's vulnerability to a lack of self-respect generally but are about the particular dangers of feelings of inferiority to and dependence on one's partner. The arguments seem to really be about the need for women to possess a self-esteem grounded in their own self-sufficiency and to achieve a level of self-respect such that they feel as valuable as their male partners. This vision of the kind and degree of self-respect that women need to possess embodies a far more substantial perfectionist vision of what constitutes a harm than does the liberal ideal that all individuals have a baseline level of self-respect.[8]

Feminists also use their vulnerability arguments selectively. They criticize certain choices because they pose high risks of certain harms but do not criticize other choices that pose equally high risks of the same harms. This selectivity suggests feminists are more concerned with the substance of the choices being made than with the risks associated with them.

For example, Okin criticizes women's choices to become full-time homemakers on the grounds the choice will make women economically vulnerable in the future. Okin suggests that women's financial dependence on their husbands makes them economically vulnerable in two ways. First, economic dependence subjects women to a lower level of income and wealth than they would have had if they had remained in the job market themselves.[9] Second, economic dependence makes women vulnerable to a sharp decline in their standard of living upon divorce.[10]

However, it is not at all clear that the choices Okin criticizes make women any more economically vulnerable than many choices Okin and other feminists do not criticize. It seems very uncertain that women who marry rich and live off their husbands, even if they at some point divorce, do not end up with more wealth over their lifetimes than they would have had if they had pursued their own careers throughout their lives and married men who were looking for less traditional women, or did not marry at all. Certainly, there is a class of women for whom the homemaking choice does involve giving up potentially lucrative career options. This is true for well-educated middle-class women with high earning potential. For most women, however, it is not clear that the choice to marry higher-earning men and become homemakers leaves them with less money over their life span than they would have had if they had chosen to continue working themselves. Feminists of course do not criticize women for forgoing wealthy marriage partners and remaining single career women.

It may also be the case that women who forgo paid employment for home-making are not more likely to suffer a sharp economic decline at some point in their lives than are those women who remain in the labor force. Upon divorce, women who are homemakers may be more likely to suffer severe economic loss than are women participating in the labor market.[11] Again, though, it is uncertain that homemakers are more likely to suffer a period of economic deprivation after divorce than are single working women upon losing their jobs. Feminists do not, however, criticize women's decisions to remain (or become) single and employed on the grounds that the choice may lead to future economic vulnerability.

A concern with economic vulnerability does not explain the selectivity of feminists' criticism of women's choices to be full-time homemakers. Feminists' real concern seems not with economic deprivation but with dependence —both financial and emotional. The concern is not with assuring a necessary level of primary goods and challenging choices that expose women to a high risk of deprivation, but with assuring a particular kind of self-respect that comes only from self-sufficiency.

Okin reveals similar perfectionist selectivity when she criticizes women's choices to become homemakers on the grounds that the choice will reduce their options in the future. Okin explains: "The skills and experience [a housewife] has gained are not valued by prospective employers. . . . Being a housewife thus both impairs a woman's ability to support herself and constrains her future choices in life."[12] However, criticizing a choice on the grounds that it leaves one with a smaller future choice set than the original set is both problematic and perfectionist.

First, every choice changes to some degree the substance of a future choice set. For example, women's choices to pursue tenure in academia shrink their choice sets in certain ways: they no longer have the option to be sex kittens for men, they cannot choose to conceptualize themselves as sex objects, and they may even lose concrete choices like the choice to have children if they cannot spare the time during the tenure track period. Yet, feminists certainly do not criticize women's choices to pursue tenure. Okin's concern, and that of other feminists, does not seem to be really with the size of women's future choice sets but with their substance.

Second, as discussed in the last chapter, the very idea that choice sets can be compared in terms of their size is troubling. It is impossible to compare the size of choice sets that contain completely different items. It is meaning-less to say that the choice set resulting from a woman's choice to be a full-time homemaker is "smaller" than the choice set resulting from a woman's choice to be a full-time professor. Vulnerability claims based on the size of future choice sets face the same problems of comparability discussed in the previous chapter.

Conclusion

When feminists challenge women's choices out of concern that the choices will make women vulnerable to future harms, the arguments at first glance may appear to be neutral about how women should live. The concern initially seems to be with promoting rational choices and preventing future liberal harms rather than with promoting a particular kind of life or conception of the good. This chapter has argued, however, that when feminists criticize women's choices on the grounds that the choices will make women vulnerable to some future harm, feminists are motivated by a distinct vision of the kinds of risks women should accept and the kinds of outcomes they should seek. This vision goes far beyond a desire to avoid liberal rights violations and embodies a more substantive conception of the activities and values that are compatible with human flourishing.

PART THREE. TOWARD A PRAGMATIC FEMINIST PERFECTIONISM

In this final part, I try to respond to the two problems that set the stage for this book: feminists' inability to challenge women's choices without resort to perfectionism, and the inadequacy of existing perfectionist theories to explain the bases of feminists' judgments. I respond by suggesting perfectionist principles that seem to underlie feminists' choice critiques. The last four chapters have argued that nonperfectionist arguments are inadequate to justify feminist criticism of women's choices to commodify their sexuality, to sexually objectify themselves, and to become full-time homemakers. As suggested in chapter 3, however, existing perfectionist theories, because of their abstraction or their focus on primary goods, do not explain and justify feminists' criticisms. This chapter both urges and presents examples of a more pragmatic perfectionism.[1]

Pragmatism disavows grand theories of truth and knowledge and focuses instead on applying theories and beliefs to particular real-life situations.[2] Pragmatists argue that while grand theories may be pretty in their coherence they are not very useful in practice. They do not serve the ultimate purpose of philosophy: presenting people with different ways to think about their own lives. Pragmatism emphasizes the importance of applying theory to real-world situations. Practical application makes theory both clear and socially relevant.

Abstract theories become comprehensible through their application to actual experiences. It is only through the "hard pragmatic work"[3] of applying rules and theories in actual situations that one understands what a theory means and requires. As John Dewey argues: "Knowledge itself must be experienced; it must be had, possessed, enacted, before it can be known."[4] It is only through concrete application that one gains a sense of the content and limits of a particular theory and of how any one theory differs from any other.

Furthermore, abstract theories only have social meaning and impact when they are applied to concrete situations. The value of a philosophical theory comes not in its abstract elegance but in what it says about different practices. Theory is important for what it tells people about how to live their lives.[5] As

William James asks: "Grant an idea or belief to be true, . . . what concrete difference will its being true make in anyone's actual life? How will the truth be realized? What experiences will be different from those which would obtain if the belief were false? What, in short, is the truth's cash-value in experiential terms?"[6]

Most of the perfectionist theories discussed in chapter 3 suffer from their own abstraction.[7] They lack both clear meaning and social impact because they fail to apply their premises to real-life events. The abstract theories suffer from what James calls "the sentimentalist fallacy." They "shed tears over abstract justice and generosity, beauty etc," yet never know what these qualities look like in practice because "the circumstances make them vulgar."[8] However, as pragmatists argue, it is the "vulgar" application of theory to practice that is the hard work of philosophy and the work that gives philosophy meaning.

Perfectionist theories seem particularly prone to otherworldly abstraction. A clearly articulated and well-grounded perfectionism, however, has much to offer philosophy and society. Developing such a perfectionism is the goal of this chapter.

My perfectionism is not a coherent abstract theory; it is a set of principles supported by empirical data and intuition. In the pragmatist tradition, I offer discrete justifications for the principles as well as discrete applications of them. I attempt with these principles to continue the hard work begun by other theorists, primarily Margaret Jane Radin and Iris Marion Young, of making perfectionism useful and applicable to people's lives. My perfectionist principles are an attempt to identify and argue on behalf of a set of beliefs about what constitutes a good human life that seems distinctly, if not always openly, present in feminist political and academic circles.

8   Four Perfectionist Principles

The previous chapters have shown that nonperfectionist arguments provide inadequate bases to justify the scope of feminists' challenge of women's choices to commodify their sexuality, objectify their sexuality, or become full-time homemakers. I have shown that nonperfectionist arguments can justify challenging only a small subset of the choices feminists commonly challenge. Furthermore, I have argued that seemingly nonperfectionist arguments often rely on perfectionist conceptions of human flourishing. This chapter seeks to uncover a pragmatic perfectionism that will avoid the historical problems with perfectionism discussed in chapter 3, yet will provide more adequate grounds for criticizing women's choices.

I argue on behalf of four perfectionist principles: (1) sexual noncommodification; (2) intellectual and moral development; (3) self-love; and (4) self-sufficiency. These principles provide a stronger and more honest basis for criticizing the kinds of choices that many feminists wish to challenge than do the seemingly neutral arguments previously discussed.

I. Sexual Noncommodification Principle

Human flourishing requires that persons be treated and conceived of as uniquely valuable and nonfungible beings. Individuals, as well as the attributes and relationships that are central to their being, should not be discussed, treated, or thought about in the same way that we discuss, treat, and think about chairs—or, at least, not only in this way. Sexuality is such a central attribute. As a result, sexual commodification degrades one's status as a human being. The sexual noncommodification principle relies on two underlying claims. The first is a claim about the nature of personhood. Sexuality is an integral and valuable part of the self. It cannot be detached from an individual and used without using the individual as a whole. The second is a claim about the nature of sexuality. Real sexuality is noncommodifiable. Commodified sexuality is simply a distortion and imitation of real sexuality; it is not the real thing. Furthermore, real sexuality is fragile. Commodified conceptions of sexuality endanger the existence of real and noncommodified conceptions.

The first claim underlying the principle against commodified sexuality is that sexuality is an essential and fully integrated part of one's being. It is inextricably linked to one's body and one's identity. Sexuality cannot be detached from a person and purchased as a separate thing or service. The purchase of a woman's sexuality involves the purchase of her whole person. Thinking of persons as things that can be purchased and used for sexual gratification degrades our conception of persons as uniquely valuable, incommensurable beings.

Margaret Jane Radin makes this argument. According to Radin, we do damage to our conception of personhood if we think of all aspects of ourselves as discrete pieces that can be separated from the whole and assessed with their own value. Certain aspects of the self are such a part of the person's core that they cannot be separated off from the rest of the person. Furthermore, "to see the rhetoric of the market—the rhetoric of fungibility, alienability, and cost-benefit analysis—as the sole rhetoric of human affairs is to foster an inferior conception of human flourishing."[1] Radin argues:

> A better view of personhood should understand many kinds of particulars —one's politics, work, religion, family, love, sexuality, friendships, altruism, experiences, wisdom, moral commitments, character and personal attributes—as integral to the self. To understand any of these as monetizable or as completely detachable from the person . . . is to do violence to our deepest understanding of what it is to be human.[2]

The inextricability of sexuality from the person as a whole is particularly clear in the case of prostitution. Prostitution involves a more total control over the whole person than do other forms of work. While other forms of physical labor may involve the worker taking orders from an employer and having her physical services at his command, they are not in his control in the same way. A football player or a factory worker can be ordered to move his body in a particular way to perform some physical feat, but the ultimate decision to do so and the ultimate control over his body remains the worker's. Sex work involves a far more substantial loss of control. Sex work involves a physical manipulation and colonization of another's body that is not seen in other forms of labor. The woman does not sell services; she sells her entire body for the temporary use of another.

Commodified sexuality involves not only the purchase and control of the whole person but also the distortion and mutation of the very quality being purchased—sexual arousal. Commodified and noncommodified sexuality are not the same attribute. Commodified sexuality is a different and less valuable distortion of sexuality; it is pretend or "as if" sexuality, not real sexuality.

Commodification distorts sexuality in the same way it distorts other attributes that are integral and essential to our sense of selves. Consider the commodification of friendship and personal beliefs. Both attributes entail certain affective and cognitive aspects in addition to typical behavioral patterns. Simply to perform the acts associated with the attribute is not to perform the attribute. The ideal versions of the attributes do not exist once the attributes are commodified because the affective and cognitive aspects that are crucial to their noncommodified versions simply cannot be bought. The valuable and "real" version of these goods only exists in noncommodified form; commodified or "as if" versions are substantively different things.

For example, friendship requires that one have some true emotional connection to another person. It requires that one wants to do things for and be with another individual because of who that individual is. Friendship is more than performing certain acts, it is more than being nice to someone, going to the movies together, and helping each other with homework—though it may well involve all of these things. Friendship requires an affective, emotive aspect that cannot be bought.[3] One cannot buy a friend; one can only buy the acts of friendship, and being a paid playmate is not the same as being a friend. Friendship simply cannot exist in commodified form as "real" friendship. Paid versions of friendship may look like friendship, they may be "as if" friendship, but they are not friendship.[4]

Personal beliefs are similar to friendships in that they too require critical internal or cognitive elements that simply cannot be bought. The capacity to evaluate an argument and to express one's genuine respect for or disagreement with an argument is central to a good human life. Yet, "real" beliefs cannot exist in commodified form. It is impossible to pay someone to believe something. It makes no sense. One can pay another to say that she believes something, or to act "as if" she believes something, but one cannot pay another person to really believe something.

The idea that there is a "real" and an "as if" version of certain personal attributes and relationships does not mean that there is only one real way to perform or experience these attributes. There may be a range or hierarchy of acceptable versions of friendship and beliefs that are all "real." The claim is only that the commodified version is not on the hierarchy because it is no longer the same thing.

Consider Aristotle's hierarchy of friendships. Some friendships are based on deeply felt caring and respect, some are based on the pleasure people have when together, and some are based on mutual self-interest or utility.[5] While the first form of friendship may be a better, more pure, more rewarding form of friendship, the other two forms are still friendship. They still possess some affective and emotional tie between the individuals.

Similarly, personal beliefs may take on a range of different forms. Some may be the result of significant research and thought, others the result of little information and thought, and still others the result of misinformation or even self-delusion. Yet all are beliefs because all involve a subjective evaluation of ideas.

There is something about sexuality, like friendship and belief, that makes commodification paradoxical and impossible. Identifying these elusive internal elements, however, is more difficult for sexuality than for the other two. "Real" sexuality requires an emotional and affective connection between two people. One acts either to bring oneself pleasure, to bring another person pleasure, or to do both. Sexuality involves more than a standard routine of physical acts. These acts can be bought, someone could be paid to perform the routine, but this is not "real" sexuality. Prostitution is like sex, it involves the acts, but it does not involve the something more that is required for "real" sexuality. As with friendships and beliefs it is this internal component that cannot be bought or sold.

Also like friendship and belief, sexuality exists in a range of different forms. Arguing that commodified sexuality is not "real" sexuality does not lead to the conclusion that only sex for love or sex for procreation is "real" sex. Sex out of lust, boredom, or friendship is also real sex. All involve some feeling of sexual arousal. Only sex for pay seems wholly lacking in the internal aspects that are essential to "real" sexuality.

However, sexual commodification does not only degrade the individual selling her sexuality and corrupt the value of the sexuality being sold. Commodification actually imperils the existence of true sexuality for all individuals.

Noncommodified conceptions of sexuality are fragile. They are weaker than their commodified counterparts. As a result, the coexistence of commodified and noncommodified conceptions of sexuality, both within the same individual and within society at large, is unstable and always in danger of falling toward exclusive commodification. Because of this fragility, sexuality should only exist in noncommodified forms.

Not all important human attributes are as fragile as sexuality. Radin, for example, argues that one's work and one's home—both of which Radin considers integral to one's sense of self—can and should be understood and treated in both commodified and noncommodified terms. Market and nonmarket rhetoric and treatment can coexist rather stably with no impending domino effect toward universal commodification.

According to Radin, while work is obviously commodified and market-driven, it is incompletely commodified because many people feel a sense of personal connectedness to and pride in their work. "The concept of the personal touch in one's work, of doing a good job for the sake of pride in one's work, for the sake of the user or recipient, and for the sake of one's community as a whole is intelligible for much of the market economy."[6] Collective-bargaining policies, minimum-wage laws, and maximum-hour requirements all reflect and reinforce society's understanding of work as something that is both a market commodity and something integral to personhood that must be protected from full market exploitation.[7]

Similarly, an individual's connection to her home has both market and nonmarket aspects. The fact that one rents or buys one's home clearly makes it a commodity. Yet, particularly after one has lived in a place for a number of years, a home takes on a value independent of its market value. It becomes a part of who one is. The home becomes part of one's personal identity.[8] Again society reflects and reinforces the coexistence of market and nonmarket visions of homes. Nonmarket aspects are reinforced through rent control, habitability requirements, and nondiscrimination laws.[9]

One's work and one's home can be thought of and treated both as commodities and as integral aspects of one's personhood. The coexistence of commodified and noncommodified versions of these goods that are central to one's sense of self seems possible and relatively stable.

In contrast, commodified and noncommodified versions of sexuality and physical personhood cannot coexist. The coexistence of dual versions of these things is highly unstable and degenerates into a universal commodification that hinders human flourishing.

As Radin argues, an active and open market in sex would hinder people's ability to think of and treat their sexuality as an emotionally connected, invaluable, and constitutive part of themselves. According to Radin:

> If sex were openly commodified in this way, its commodification would
> be reflected in everyone's discourse about sex, and in particular about
> women's sexuality. New terms would emerge for particular gradations of
> sexual market value. New discussions would be heard of particular abilities
> or qualities in terms of their market value. With this change in discourse,
> when it became pervasive enough, would come a change in everyone's
> experience, because experience is discourse dependent.[10]

The sexual noncommodification principle asserts that noncommodified sexuality is fundamental to personhood, and the very existence of commodified conceptions of sexuality threatens to destroy it. In order to make this principle pragmatic, the next question is: What activities does the principle of sexual noncommodification counsel against?

The remainder of this section will consider different activities in light of this principle. As argued in the preceding chapters, nonperfectionist arguments can justify challenging only a small subset of the ways in which women choose to commodify their sexuality. They provide a basis to challenge only those decisions made in response to threatened rights violations. The noncommodification principle provides a basis for challenging a broader range of sexual commodification choices that many feminists find problematic.

Most obviously, the principle against sexual commodification challenges the compatibility of prostitution with a meaningful human life. In prostitution the purchase of a woman's sexuality most clearly involves the purchase of the whole woman. Prostitution involves not merely the purchase of services that the woman performs, or the purchase of a thing that can be separated from her body. It involves the purchase of her whole body and being. Prostitution involves the physical control of and use of a woman's body and sexuality. The woman does not simply respond to directions of what to do with her body; her body is acted upon and used in the desired ways. No other form of work involves such a complete control of a person's being.[11] Moreover, what is bought is not real sex. The woman's real sexuality is not—and cannot be—bought. What is purchased is the use of the woman's body and her willingness to go through the physical motions of sex. Her arousal, passion, and emotion are not purchasable acts or things.

Furthermore, this commodified version of sex endangers the ability of women and men to conceptualize and engage in noncommodified sex by imposing a monetary conception on the sexuality and selves of all persons. Once people think of their sexuality as a thing that can be separated and bought from them, it makes a pure noncommodified conception and experience of their sexuality difficult. Merely knowing the dollar value of one's sexuality and what one could sell it for on the market, like knowing one's value on a slave auction block, makes it impossible to conceive of oneself as unique, invaluable, and nonfungible. Sexual commodification, in the form of prostitution, imperils our conception of ourselves and others as fully human beings.

According to the sexual noncommodification principle, all forms of prostitution are incompatible with human flourishing. The noncommodification principle is not limited—as the nonperfectionist arguments are—to criticizing only those choices that result from traditional forms of coercion. Because most feminists who find women's choices to enter prostitution problematic do not limit their criticism to prostitution that is coerced in the traditional sense, the noncommodification principle provides a more accurate basis for their criticism than do the nonperfectionist arguments more commonly relied on.

The noncommodification principle does not, however, justify the same criticism of other forms of sexual commodification. Consider lap dancing, which generally involves a scantily clad or naked woman shimmying on the lap of a male customer. In lap dancing, as in prostitution, what is being sold is some relationship with or interaction with a woman's pretend sexuality. Lap dancing, however, differs from prostitution in two ways that make it less offensive to the sexual noncommodification principle. First, lap dancing involves a less complete purchase of the woman's sexuality. Unlike prostitution, where the woman's body is being bought and used in the most literal way, lap dancing maintains a greater distinction between the woman's self and what is actually for sale. Lap dancing generally involves rules prohibiting a customer from actively touching the woman who is rubbing up against him. This prohibition against a customer reaching out and maneuvering or controlling the woman's body during the dance raises a critical distinction between lap dancing and prostitution. What is for sale in lap dancing looks less like the woman's very being and self and more like a particular service. Lap dancing looks more like the sale of other services—such as massage, and car washing—than does prostitution. While the service for sale in lap dancing is decidedly erotic, it remains possible to distinguish the sale of the sexual service from the sale of the woman. Lap dancers sell a performance that they control rather than selling control over themselves. Lap dancing poses less threat than prostitution of rendering a woman a sexual object that can be bought for a man's pleasure and use.

Lap dancing also seems to pose less danger to an idealized noncommodified conception of sexuality. At a high level of specificity, the existence of commodified lap dancing does not drive out or endanger noncommodified versions and conceptions of lap dancing. One might argue that my level of comparison is too specific. Commodified lap dancing may not endanger a noncommodified socially valuable conception of lap dancing, but it may endanger noncommodified conceptions of sexuality more generally. This is a danger. The sale of any sexual services contributes to some extent to our view of sexuality as a good with a market value. However, the more that lap dancing looks like the sale of services rather than the sale of a woman, the less dangerous it seems to our noncommodified conceptions of both women and sexuality.

Pornography presents a difficult issue for the noncommodification princip-le. At least with respect to the protection of personhood, pornography looks more like lap dancing than it looks like prostitution. I assume that some women participate in pornography without being coerced in any tradi-tional sense. Coerced pornography is easy to criticize—if not to stop—on nonperfectionist grounds. However, women participating in pornography ab-sent the threat of physical violence retain a greater degree of control over their sexuality and selves than do those in prostitution. Pornography involves less of a complete sale of the woman's sexuality and body and looks more like the sale of services meant to be sexually arousing for the buyer. The pornographic actress may be told what to do with her body and what positions to take, but ultimately it is she who takes the positions and moves her body, or chooses not to.

Much of the opposition to pornography, most notably that of Catharine MacKinnon, has focused on the fragility of noncommodified conceptions of sexuality in the face of bombardment by commodified versions of pornogra-phy. The fragility question raises the same degree-of-specificity issue that was raised by lap dancing. Is the concern that pornographic modeling for money will make impossible pornographic modeling for pleasure, or that commodi-fied pornography will make impossible noncommodified conceptions of sex more generally? I think no one is particularly concerned that commodified pornography might make some socially valuable noncommodified version of pornography impossible. The real concern is that commodified pornography will have a detrimental effect on noncommodified conceptions of sex more generally.

Although I discounted the fragility argument with respect to lap dancing, the concern seems more significant with respect to pornography probably be-cause of the far greater prevalence of pornography and because it serves an educative role that lap dancing does not. Pornography may be incompatible with human flourishing less because of what it does to the individual actor's personhood—I have argued that pornography involves less of a purchase of the self than does prostitution—and more for what it does to all individuals' ability to enjoy noncommodified sex.[12] Pornography may, therefore, under-mine human flourishing not because of what it does to those who participate in it directly as actors or models but because of what it does to all of us who learn how to conceive of and experience our sexuality through pornography. Pornography teaches women and men that women are for men's sexual use and pleasure. Pornography reduces women to their sexuality and strips their sexuality of any connection to a whole person. Women's sexuality is not an integrated part of their personhood. Instead, women's sexuality is both all they are and all they are for. Pornography, in its role as sex educator, endangers our ability to conceive of and experience sexuality as an integrated part of a fully human self-conception.

Participation in fashion modeling raises issues similar to those raised by pornography. Fashion modeling sells not only designer clothes, but also the pretend sexuality of the model. Like pornography, however, fashion modeling seems to pose less of a threat to the personhood of the model than does prostitution. The woman's sexuality and body are not being bought and controlled in the literal form that exists in prostitution. The woman remains in control of her actions and her body. She is directed on what to do and how to look, but ultimately it is still the woman owning and controlling herself. Fashion modeling looks more like other forms of labor than does prostitution. Fashion modeling looks like car washing or retail clothing sales; it looks more like the sale of services than the sale of the person.

Fashion modeling also raises issues similar to those of pornography with respect to the fragility of noncommodified conceptions of sexuality more generally. As with pornography, fashion modeling does not exist in an idealized noncommodified form that is endangered by the presence of a commodified form of fashion modeling. At a higher level of generality, however, one could argue that fashion modeling endangers our idealized noncommodified conception of sexuality. Just as pornography endangers our conception of ourselves as uniquely valuable integrated beings by teaching us that women can be bought and used as sexual objects, fashion modeling sends a similar, though perhaps less stark message. Fashion modeling, like pornography, teaches women and men that women are interchangeable beauty objects. The lesson of fashion modeling seems to be more about women's value as beauty objects than it is about their value as objects for sex per se. That is, while pornography teaches women and men that women are for purchase and use for sex, fashion modeling teaches primarily that women are for social decoration (decoration which is often erotic or sensually arousing). While pornography may endanger women's ability to conceive of and experience their sexuality as an integrated part of a uniquely valuable whole being, fashion modeling may endanger women's ability to conceive of themselves as other than decorative chairs.

II. Intellectual and Moral Development Requirement

A second requirement for a full human life is the exercise of abstract reason and the development of a sense of impersonal social justice. At least in liberal democracies, the means by which individuals develop and exer-

cise these capacities is normally through some form of public-sphere participation.

Iris Marion Young, for example, stresses the importance of developing and
exercising one's capacity for abstract rationality and one's sense of social justice by interacting with impersonal others in one's social community. Says
Young, "Citizenship is an expression of the universality of human life; it is a
realm of rationality and freedom as opposed to the heteronomous realm of
particular need, interest, and desire."[13] Participation in the political life of
one's community encourages important cognitive development. "In partici-
patory democratic institutions citizens develop and exercise capacities of reasoning, discussion, and socializing that otherwise lie dormant, and they move
out of their private existence to address others and face them with respect
and concern for justice."[14]

Given that real political participation, in any form greater than voting, is
extremely rare among women as well as men, this second perfectionist principle calls for public-sphere participation more broadly. Through public-
sphere participation individuals develop abstract reason and a sense of social
justice. Interacting regularly with other persons with whom an individual
does not have close or intense personal ties forces her to recognize the ways
in which she is similar to and different from these multiple others, and, most
importantly, it forces her to recognize that she is only one among many, all of
whom have different wants and desires, and all of whom are deserving of the
same degree of social respect and attention.

By participating in public organizations one develops a realistic picture of
one's own social and historical importance, of the value of lives generally, and
of the value of one's own life. Individuals must participate in the public
sphere in order to understand their place within a large, impersonal, and
rather abstract social context.

The difficulty for any perfectionist theory is always in translating from
theory to practice. What degree and kind of public-sphere participation is
necessary to produce these essential intellectual and emotional states? What
life choices are and are not compatible with this requirement for human
flourishing?

The public-sphere participation needed to satisfy the second perfectionist
principle entails regular ongoing interaction, negotiation, discussion, and debate with a group of people devoted to a common mission that has some effect on individuals outside of the organization. It requires being a part of an
organization that is committed in some way to how the larger society works.
The organization may want to change the drinking age, or get people to buy

more bleach, but in some way it is concerned about and involved with a community that is larger than just its immediate members.

The most obvious and common form of public-sphere participation is paid employment. Work forces one to maintain numerous superficial acquaintances with people of different backgrounds, beliefs, and values.[15] Membership in this rather impersonal whole helps a person to conceive of her place in a large heterogeneous society and to develop a sense of abstract and impersonal justice.

Public-sphere participation that is not in the form of paid employment may provide the same intellectual and emotional benefits. For example, volunteer activities such as the Junior League, the PTA (Parent-Teacher Association), or the League of Women Voters may provide individuals with the requisite amount of public-sphere activity to enable them think abstractly about their community and their world and to provide an adequate balance to the intense private-sphere relationships that make them so emotionally vulnerable. The key with volunteer work is that one must be suitably committed to it both in terms of time and emotional attachment in order to reap these rewards. Stuffing envelopes three hours a month for the League of Women Voters is probably not enough for one to develop a sense of abstract social justice. Working twenty hours a week with one's school board, superintendent, and local teachers on behalf of the PTA to develop a new reading curriculum probably is.

This perfectionist requirement for human flourishing challenges choices women have traditionally made that remove them from meaningful public-sphere participation and seclude them in the domestic sphere. Particularly dangerous from this perspective are choices made by young women who marry after graduating from high school and then devote themselves full-time and wholeheartedly to raising children and caring for their husband and home. Many of these women probably never fully develop their capacities for abstract thinking that come from interacting with and making decisions that impact those outside one's own immediate affective and particularistic knowledge base.

III. Self-Love Requirement

The third perfectionist principle centers on the idea of self-love. One must think of and treat oneself as a being whose interests, preferences, wants, and desires are as valuable and worthy of satisfaction as those of all other persons. Each individual must love herself to the same extent that she loves and values others. This is essentially a reversal of Kant's practical imperative with a twist. Kant's practical imperative holds that one must treat all other people not simply as means but also as ends.[16] One must never treat another person solely as an instrument for the satisfaction of one's own ends or desires but must always recognize and treat the other person as a being with her own valuable ends. The Kantian reversal involved in this perfectionist principle is that instead of requiring that one recognize and treat others as ends and never solely as means, it requires that one never treat oneself merely as a means but also always as an end. One must never conceive of and treat oneself merely as an instrument or object existing for someone else's pleasure, satisfaction, care, or anger. Instead, one must always recognize one's own independent goals and values. The twist on the Kantian categorical imperative is that in addition to treating herself as an end, a woman must treat herself and her goals as being as important and worthy of attention and care from herself and from the rest of society as anyone else's.

Satisfying this perfectionist principle requires meaningful self-reflective deliberation. One must have ends that are in some way truly one's own—ends that reflect deeply held personal desires or promote one's own happiness. It is not enough to simply adopt as one's ends those of one's husband or child. Each individual must value herself as much as she values anyone else and must struggle to determine her own ends rather than simply adopting some-one else's. Determining when an individual is pursuing her own ends from a position of self-love and valuation and when one is simply accepting another person's aims as her own, because she feels that the other person is more im-portant, is not easy.[17] Consider the difference between two women who follow their husbands' career moves. One woman leaves her job and moves with her husband because she believes that her husband's career is more important than her own and that whatever is best for her husband is definitionally best for her. The other woman leaves her job when her husband is relocated be-cause she wants the family to stay together, because the last family move was made for her job advancement, and because she will gain the pleasure and the satisfaction of acting fairly if she makes this move in order to further his ca-reer. The self-love requirement is probably satisfied by the second woman but not the first. In the first scenario the woman has simply absorbed the ends and goals of her husband rather than developing her own.

In practice, the self-love principle leads to criticism of women's choices to objectify themselves sexually and to become full-time homemakers. Women who conceive of themselves as beauty objects for male enjoyment and who derive their sense of personal worth from their value as gaze objects necessarily lack the self-love described here. Gaze objects do not have any value independent of that attributed to them by their viewers. Not only is the objectified woman defined by and valued by her observers but she also takes on their ends as her own. Her end is the voyeur's aesthetic pleasure. The sex object is wholly dependent on the observer for her value and purpose. She does not have the independent assessment of self-worth and purpose necessary for the self-love requirement.

Similarly, women who become homemakers and are financially dependent on their husbands are likely to be less powerful in the relationship than their husbands. Financial and psychological dependence on another gradually teaches that the dependent spouse's desires and goals are less important than those of the provider. The dependent spouse both learns that her ends are less important than her spouse's and learns to incorporate the provider's ends as her own in order to minimize her subjective experience of domination.

IV. Self-Sufficiency Requirement

The fourth perfectionist principle is that an individual must have the ability to support herself financially at a level which she finds acceptable and not frightening. This requirement, which seems so simple and superficial, may in fact be the most important requirement of the four.[18] The capability for self-subsistence is critical for self-determination, and for one's sense of stability, security, and self-respect. As I previously argued, this concern with ensuring that individuals possess self-respect grounded in self-sufficiency underlies many of feminists' vulnerability-based arguments.

One must have the capability for self-support at an acceptable level in order to have the independence, security, and confidence necessary for a good human life. The capacity for self-sufficiency ensures that one has a viable exit option from relationships that are dangerous, painful, or unpleasant.

One need not actually be self-supporting at all moments of life. What is important for human flourishing is the knowledge that one could support oneself, and one's dependents.[19]

The importance of self support for dignity, self-determination, and freedom of expression has not been overlooked by women over the centuries. Women, having been traditionally denied the ability to support themselves financially, have recognized the numerous ways that financial dependence impedes human flourishing.

In the eighteenth century Mary Wollstonecraft decried women's total social and economic dependence on men. She argued that dependence weakened women's minds and souls, rendering them both powerless and manipulative. Women's full citizenship and development required that they be educated and permitted to be self-sufficient. According to Wollstonecraft:

> If marriage be the cement of society, mankind should all be educated after the same model, or the intercourse of the sexes will never deserve the name of fellowship, nor will women ever fulfill the peculiar duties of their sex, till they become enlightened citizens, till they become free by being enabled to earn their own subsistence, independent of men.[20]

In the nineteenth century, Harriet Taylor Mill and John Stuart Mill also stressed the importance of financial independence for women's self development and self-respect. According to Taylor Mill and Mill:

> The first and indispensable step, therefore, towards the enfranchisement of woman, is that she be so educated, as not to be dependent either on her father or her husband for subsistence: a position which in nine cases out of ten, makes her either the plaything or the slave of the man who feeds her; and in the tenth case, only his humble friend.[21]

They argued that just as men considered it degrading to depend on another's kind feelings for their survival, so too was such dependence degrading for women: "[M]en think it base and servile in men to accept food as the price of dependence, and why do they not deem it so in women? solely because they do not desire that women should be their equals."[22]

While Taylor Mill and Mill agreed that women needed to be able to support themselves through paid labor, they disagreed on whether women should in fact do so. It was Taylor Mill who took the stronger, more radical position of the two by arguing that women should actually be economically independent throughout their adult lives. Taylor Mill argued that "[e]ven if every woman . . . had a claim on some man for support, how infinitely preferable is it that part of the [couple's] income should be of the woman's earning . . . rather than that she should be compelled to stand aside in order that men may be the sole earners, and the sole dispensers of what is earned."[23] Mill, in turn, wanted to ensure that women had access to the professions, though he still assumed and encouraged a traditional division of labor within the family. According to Mill:

> Like a man when he chooses a profession, so, when a woman marries, it may in general be understood that she makes choice of the management of a household, and the bringing up of a family, as the first call upon her exertions, during as many years of her life as may be required for the purpose;

and that she renounces, not all other objects and occupations, but all which are not consistent with the requirements of this.[24]

The need for self-sufficiency and financial independence for a fully human life was repeated again in the twentieth century by Virginia Woolf. In both *A Room of One's Own* and *Three Guineas,* Woolf stressed the importance of financial independence for intellectual freedom, creativity, and self-determination. In *A Room of One's Own,* Woolf explained that in order to have, develop, and express one's thoughts, one needed both financial independence and a quiet place of one's own. In order to write fiction or poetry, Woolf concluded that "it is necessary to have five hundred [pounds] a year and a room with a lock on the door."[25] Women, of course, have historically been without either.

In *Three Guineas,* Woolf stresses the importance of financial independence in allowing women to hold and act on their own judgments rather than mimicking the opinions of those on whom they are dependent. In the face of impending war, Woolf argued that women needed financial independence from their husbands so they could oppose men's cries for war. She argued that the state paying women wages for marriage and motherhood as professions was "the most effective way in which we can ensure that the large and very honourable class of married women shall have a mind and a will of their own."[26] Woolf, like Taylor Mill and Mill, reminded men that, just as they would find their own financial dependence on another individual degrading, such dependence is equally degrading for women. As Woolf instructed a male correspondent, "You will agree, sir, . . . that to depend upon [your wife] for your income would effect a most subtle and undesirable change in your psychology."[27]

Woolf was certainly right. The significance of independence and self-sufficiency for men has almost mythic dimensions. Men know that their lives are less meaningful if they cannot provide for themselves; their self-worth depends on their independence. In America manhood and masculinity are closely tied to a man's ability to support himself and his family. Anthropologist David Gilmore suggests that this emphasis is crosscultural. "To know a man, to judge him as a man . . . you have to see him at work at useful jobs; you have to know his energy quotient as a worker, a producer, a builder. Work defines manhood, but not just work as energy spent but as labor that supports life, constructive labor."[28]

Strangely though, discussion about the importance of being self-sufficient and independent is largely absent from traditional political theory. It seems to be simply taken for granted. Both Locke and Rousseau just assume that men have the capability to earn their own living. In fact, what drives men into social compacts, according to both theorists, is a need for men to protect the goods and property they accumulate through their labors. No time is wasted arguing, as the feminist theorists had to, about the importance of being able to earn and own the products of one's labor and the source of one's subsistence.[29]

As a practical matter, the fourth perfectionist principle challenges women's choices to remove themselves wholly from public-sphere activities, to neglect whatever marketable skills they may once have had, and to become wholly financially dependent on a spouse. For example, imagine a forty-year-old homemaker with three children. She has spent the last twenty years of her life developing highly specialized knowledge and skills. She knows what foods her children like and dislike, how to help each child fall back asleep after having a nightmare, and how to make each member of her family feel better when they are sad. This information makes her highly valued by her particular family, but it does not make her very valuable or marketable in the public sphere of paid employment. Although the woman did graduate from college before getting married and starting a family, since then she has only held occasional part-time positions paying close to minimum wage. She has not developed or maintained the marketable skills she once had. On her forty-first birthday her husband tells her he wants a divorce. He's having a midlife crisis and he wants to start over with another twenty-three-year-old. The woman is left with child support, a divorce settlement, and, if she is both lucky and unusual, temporary alimony payments. The woman is also left with no viable and foreseeable options to provide for herself and her children at the level to which they were accustomed: a standard middle-class life. The woman's standard of living drops precipitously and she and her children become members of one of the fastest-growing groups living in poverty today. The woman has lost the security, stability, and consistency needed for a good human life.

However, even if this scenario never plays out—even if the woman's husband never leaves her—the very knowledge that one's well-being depends entirely on another person's continued financial support and generosity undermines one's self-determination and imposes some degree of hierarchy into one's relationship with one's provider. Such dependence on another individual for one's survival breeds an insecurity and servility that is incompatible with human flourishing.

As stated earlier, this principle of self-sufficiency does not require that one be at all moments self supporting, only that one has the capability of becoming so in a manner one finds acceptable. Imagine a second woman who has also devoted herself full-time to homemaking for the last twenty years but who has also been volunteering for the last ten years in her children's school as a computer aide. She teaches students new computer programs, shows them how to surf the Internet, and helped the school set up its own Web page. The woman was a computer science major in college and does her volunteer work to keep her knowledge current and to keep herself marketable. She knows that she could enter the labor market and find well-paid work rather easily given the high demand for workers with computer skills. Because of her public-sphere options the woman has a sense of security and stability about her life that the first woman lacks. This woman knows that her lifestyle cannot be taken away from her by the whim of another individual. She can maintain the standard of living that she desires. This woman also has more control over her life and her personal relations. Her marriage does not rest on the perhaps unspoken truth that whatever the breadwinner wants badly enough he gets, because his spouse has no bargaining power with which to stop him.[30] This woman knows, and her spouse knows, that she can always leave the relationship and support herself if they cannot work out a compromise acceptable to both. Her threats become credible because of her self-sufficiency.

One might argue that this focus on self-subsistence is peculiarly American, that it reflects a liberal individualism too particular to American culture to be considered a universal principle of human flourishing. One might argue that this need for self-sufficiency is far less important in societies that foster and expect a far greater degree of interdependence among all persons.

However, even in cultures where there is a greater emphasis on familial interdependence and responsibility for one's kin, individuals still need to be able to provide for their own and their dependents' subsistence. Sole dependence on family members, be it on a spouse or on one's in-laws, for one's survival is demeaning, frightening, and incompatible with self-determination.

Martha Chen's study of women in rural Bangladesh and India makes clear that the capability for self-sufficiency is as important in cultures where there is a strong emphasis on kinship bonds as it is in more individualistic societies like the United States. Chen describes the plight of two women—one whose husband was injured, the other whose husband died—who were left to fend for themselves and their children. Both women were bound by custom not to leave their homes and not to participate in the labor market. Both women were dependent upon the inadequate aid of their relatives and faced destitution and starvation. One woman broke from the norms of her culture and sought market employment in order to survive; the other, as of Chen's writing, had yet to do so and faced a bleak future. Chen makes clear that even in cultures that may seem less individualistic, more family-oriented, and more interdependent than our own, having the capability to support and provide for oneself and one's dependents is a fundamental requirement for the security, stability, and control necessary for a good human life.[31]

The self-sufficiency principle encourages individuals to have a capacity for self-support that does not depend upon maintaining a particular kind of relationship with a particular other individual.[32] Obviously some people can be self-sufficient and economically independent without working in the public sphere. Those who are rich and can live comfortably off their trust funds may have no need for either labor-market participation or a relationship of dependence. Similarly, if one lived in a society that provided comfortable wages for housework and child care, one could also avoid traditional public-sphere market participation without becoming dependent upon another individual.[33] The narrow focus of this requirement is on one's capability for economic independence. There may, of course, be other reasons, as suggested by the previous perfectionist principles, why lives lived exclusively off one's trust fund or off state welfare checks may be less in keeping with a good human life than lives spent participating and earning one's living in the public sphere.

Conclusion

The four perfectionist principles I have described and tried to apply seem to underlie and explain a great deal of the feminist criticism of women's real-life choices. I describe these principles less to convince the reader that these values are true keys to human flourishing and more to identify openly the values that seem to motivate and define much of current feminist discourse. The purpose of the chapter is to encourage feminists to openly acknowledge their hidden values and perfectionism and to spur debate among feminists and others about competing conceptions of the good.

9 Conclusion

This book has sought to assess the dogma of contemporary academic and political feminism in order to uncover a feminist agenda that academic feminists generally deny exists, yet one by which most ordinary women feel they are judged. This book has examined feminists' attempts to criticize women's choices in neutral liberal terms, which effectively make such criticism seem more palatable, less radical, and most importantly, less judgmental. Beneath such neutrality, however, lurks something of a hidden agenda, whose open exposition is now essential to bring women closer to a more substantive social equality with men. In other words, somewhat paradoxically, what feminists fear to say is precisely what they need to say in order to advance gender equality. With that in mind, this book has two distinct agendas: first, to defend perfectionism as a necessary foundation for contemporary feminist political theory; and second, to argue on behalf of a particular version of perfectionism.

There is little doubt that liberal procedural arguments which focus on ensuring that all individuals possess equal rights and have equal access to the public sphere of society have been largely responsible for the strides American women have made to date: access to jobs, schools, juries, and the right to equal pay. Liberalism's focus on formal legal equality both justifies and requires women's treatment as full and equal public citizens. Much of women's continued subjugation must, therefore, be attributed to the different choices women and men make about how to structure their career and family lives in a society in which both have formally equal options. Because women's choices leave them generally poorer, less skilled, and less confident than men, women's choices are a source of feminist concern and are the focus of this book.

Liberalism is in some ways a powerful and in other ways a nonthreatening political ideology. It requires political and legal equality without requiring or even advocating that individuals pursue any particular kinds of projects or activities. Liberalism can get and has gotten women in many industrialized democracies political and social rights and formal legal equality with men. Liberalism's neutrality toward private conceptions of the good, however, means that liberalism provides no guidance or instruction for how women should take advantage of their new opportunities. Liberalism's neutrality prevents it from encouraging women's substantive equality because it cannot advocate for better choices by women. Liberalism cannot encourage women to think about themselves and their lives in particular ways.

This book has focused on three particular choices that are all integral to women's continued social subordination yet are largely unchallengeable in liberal terms. The choices are harmful for women as individuals and for women's status as a group, yet liberalism cannot explain why or justify social discouragement of the choices. There are good and powerful reasons why women's choices to commodify their sexuality, to objectify their sexuality, and to become full-time homemakers make feminists apprehensive. The reasons, however, are simply nonliberal.

Sexual commodification not only reduces the woman being sold to an object for another person's sexual gratification, but it reinforces the idea that all women can be bought and used as sexual objects. Because women are seen more widely as sexual objects than as intellectual ones, sexual commodification of some women teaches all women that their greatest social value is as sex objects for men's pleasure. Similarly, sexual objectification leads to the atrophy of one's sense of self, one's independence, and one's self-worth. The worth of a sex object is not internal and self-determined but external and other-determined. Full-time homemaking is probably the most controversial of the choices discussed in this book. The choice exaggerates women's role as helper and nurturer for others, hinders women's development of independent skills and ambitions, and renders women wholly dependent on and vulnerable to the men for whom they are giving care.

As discussed in part II of this book, what is problematic about these choices cannot be described in liberal and neutral terms. While liberalism generally sanctifies individual choice and accords it high respect, there is a certain category of choices that liberalism has no trouble treating as illegitimate. Liberalism guarantees to all individuals freedom, bodily integrity, and autonomy to choose their own life path. Choices that are freely made are entitled to a great deal of social deference. However, choices that are made in response to traditional forms of coercion are considered not "real" choices and are illegitimate. The woman's choice made in response to the mugger's threat of "Your money or your life" is not a "real" choice. The threat violates liberalism's guarantee of basic bodily integrity. The "choice" is considered illegitimate and the decision maker is not bound by it once the threat to her life is over. Should the police later find the mugger and the wallet, the wallet still legally belongs to the woman rather than the mugger despite her decision to hand it over. Liberalism can easily criticize and delegitimate a small group of choices made in response to traditional coercion. Other than this narrow set of choices, however, liberalism respects and protects individual choices.

The choices described in this book cannot be criticized by relying on liberal anti-coercion arguments because they are most often not the product of traditional forms of coercion. At least some women are not forced by traditional means into prostitution, but make the choice based on the same set of basically legitimate, albeit constrained, pressures and concerns that cause people to make other decisions. Women most often self-objectify not because they are forced to, or have no other option, but because they learn early in life the rewards that being a pretty object can bring: attention, gifts, friends, wealth, and security. Being a full-time homemaker, too, is overwhelmingly not something women are forced to do but something women want very much to do. It fulfills a cultural ideal and alleviates a socially exacerbated guilt over not giving one's children one's full attention. It also frees one from having to compete and possibly fail in the public sphere.

The arguments that feminists use to criticize and challenge these choices necessarily move beyond a focus on traditional coercion. Feminists expand the concept of coercion to argue that decisions made in response to particularly difficult choices are "coerced" and unfree in the same way as the woman's choice to hand over her wallet in response to the mugger's threat. Feminists also challenge these choices by pointing to the gendered socialization of girls and boys, and to the different choices women and men face throughout their lives. Alternatively, they criticize the choices because they will leave women economically worse off in the future.

All these arguments have necessarily moved away from any real claim to being neutral about the substance of people's lives and choices. Arguments that women should not be faced with certain "seductive offers," that girls and boys should be socialized to desire certain kinds of lives, that women and men should face the same choices even in areas where there are relevant differences between the two, and that women should not accept certain kinds of risks, are all arguments motivated by a particular vision of how women should live their lives that goes far beyond liberalism's simple guarantee of basic rights to all individuals. This book has sought to uncover and advocate the vision of the good life motivating feminists' criticisms of women's choices.

Although this book's title refers to "contemporary feminist values," there is, of course, no unified set of feminist values. Particularly on the issue of prostitution and sexual commodification more generally, there is a great deal of disagreement among feminists on how these choices should be treated. I have tried to make this disagreement clear in chapter 2. With respect to the choices to self-objectify and to become full-time homemakers, there is less dissent among feminists from the general opposition to these choices levied by academic feminists. This book has focused on and tried to distill the feminist opposition to all three choices discussed in this book. It has tried to tease out and defend the values underlying much, though certainly not all, contemporary feminist writing.

The book seeks, of course, not only to uncover feminists' hidden perfectionist values, and to argue that perfectionism is crucial to women's improved social status, but to make these values useful through application. It is one thing to have vague values about how people should live, and it is something entirely different to know whether the values counsel in favor of option X or option Y when presented with a particular choice. I have tried to make clear the scope and impact of the perfectionist principles I endorsed in the last chapter. I have argued that a principle against sexual commodification rejects prostitution as a worthwhile endeavor but does not necessarily also reject fashion modeling, and does not require an ideal version of having sex only for love. I have argued that intellectual and moral development requires some form of regular public-sphere participation in order for individuals to develop a sense of impartial and abstract justice, but it does not require that all women become philosophers or even that they all hold full-time jobs. I have argued that the principle of self-love rejects self-objectification and full-time homemaking decisions for women because both normally involve women being defined by and dependent for their well-being on men. The principle does not, however, make impossible acts of freely chosen altruism for one's family or others. Finally, the principle of self-sufficiency requires that women have some means of supporting themselves, but does not require women do so at all times.

The implications of moving toward a more open perfectionist debate are significant. The most critical advantage of such a move is that the debate will necessarily lead to a stronger, more thoughtfully considered set of arguments about why certain choices women make should be discouraged. An open dialogue will be more likely to offend those women and men who disagree with the values being espoused, but it will also be more likely to convince those who are exposed to the arguments head-on. By bringing feminist perfectionist arguments outside the liberal closet and exposing them in public debate, feminists will be able to see how they survive and which assumptions need to be rethought.

Moreover, an open discussion of feminist values will allow for advocacy of political and social change in the strongest and most honest terms. Values are a key part of many types of political debates, from community discussions about what school textbooks to choose to national discussions about how to shape welfare-reform measures. All of these political discussions are at root driven by some notion of our collective social values, with changes in policies over the years reflecting our changing values.

There is no reason why feminists' values should be absent from the political forum. Christian and conservative values are advocated openly and to great effect. For feminists to achieve the kinds of changes needed for substantive equality, feminist values must be advocated as well.

An open endorsement of a feminist perfectionism might, for example, lead to a policy in elementary through high schools of not only giving girls the opportunity to compete with boys in math, science, and athletics, but of openly encouraging girls' participation. A number of policies, such as girls-only math classes, teacher training designed to make sure teachers focus equal attention on girls and boys, and strongly enforced rules against sexual harassment of students by students or teachers, might be called for by a more open valuation of girls' intellectual development and social participation. To the extent that sexual objectification is deemed to be a less valuable pursuit than intellectual development, schools might try to eliminate or at least make less attractive the most compelling sex-kitten options for young girls. Schools might get rid of their all-girl cheerleading squad and replace it with a more general, less elitist and non-gender-based cheer team. Schools might also get rid of any beauty-pageant-type rituals like selection of a homecoming or prom queen. Schools might also impose a uniform on students in order to discourage girls' emphasis on their clothes and appearance.

On a national level a social adoption of feminist values might inform the debate over whether welfare mothers should be required to work while their children are young. Placing a value on social and financial independence and skill development would counsel in favor of requiring women to work outside the home, develop marketable skills, and become, whenever possible, self-sufficient. An endorsement of more conservative family-oriented values, in contrast, might counsel for the reverse and would encourage welfare policies where the government pays to allow women to stay home full-time with their young children. Feminist values might also encourage changes in state divorce laws. The current trend is to treat women and men equally in the case of divorce. Feminist values encouraging individual development would support policies promoting women's and men's equal sharing of child custody and child care responsibilities. Feminist values might also have something to say about how states structure the division of property upon divorce as well as each partner's access to the other's income during marriage, though it is not clear precisely where feminist values would lead. On the one hand, a value of individual accomplishment and independence might encourage policies in which each member of a couple retains control over her or his income during marriage and can buy property in her or his own name without the other having any claim to it. Upon divorce, each might be entitled to only that income and wealth which she or he actually contributed to the couple. Alternatively, a focus on avoiding women's psychological and financial dependence on men might lead to a very different set of policies. It might encourage policies such as those suggested by Susan Okin, where the wages earned during a marriage are legally owned and controlled by both parties, and where upon divorce the higher-earning spouse must continue to provide for the lower-earning spouse at the standard of living to which they have both become accustomed.[1]

The point is that values are already an integral part of our policy making, and in fact many, if not most, political and policy decisions cannot be made absent questions about social values. Feminist values should more openly enter the political fray and join the social debate about how public policy should be oriented and organized.

Political influence notwithstanding, feminist perfectionism would probably have its greatest impact not in the realm of formal politics but in the realm of informal interpersonal contacts. A more open feminist dialogue about the kinds of life choices that are and are not compatible with a meaningful life could penetrate the daily lives and daily choices of individuals. At the individual level, an open feminist perfectionism could have a profound and widespread impact on how individual women structure their lives. It would also give women and men help in articulating why they think their friends may be making bad choices and give them ammunition to try to change their friends' minds.

Ultimately, feminist perfectionism can affect policy and individual thinking in ways that liberalism is unable to. Perfectionism can allow feminists to argue openly for the policy changes and the changes in individual thinking that are essential to improving the quality of individual women's lives and the status of women as a group.

As mentioned in the introduction, an endorsement or advocacy of perfectionism scares people. The fear, of course, is of a totalitarian perfectionist state enforcing some kind of homogeneous ideal—perhaps requiring all girls to become mathematicians or physicians. While there are dangers in moving away from liberalism as the dominant mode of feminist discourse, the dangers of a feminist totalitarian regime are unreal. The feminist perfectionism advocated in this book does not encourage a single ideal. Instead, it advocates a plural perfectionism that includes many different types of lives and activities and simply discourages a limited set of activities as degrading.

The point of feminist perfectionism is not to impose a single way of life on people, but to put forth feminists' best arguments in the hopes of persuading people to pursue certain activities over others. If the arguments are convincing, they will work themselves into policy through the standard modes of the democratic process. Values are already part of politics, and there is nothing insidious about having feminist values join the fray.

There are, however, risks in changing the language of social debate from one based on liberal terms and on liberal concepts to one focusing openly and directly on values. The danger is that individuals with different values will simply be unable to communicate with each other; they will have no common ground or shared understanding. Liberalism provides a common language with which individuals who hold different moral and religious views can communicate on social and political issues. Liberalism provides a diverse society with a framework within which to debate issues.

In a liberal society, social debates start from the premise that individuals are all equally worthy of social care and respect and immutable characteristics such as race and sex cannot justify depriving any individual or group of individuals of their basic social rights. Moreover, arguments must be based on theories of social justice and human nature, or on empirical or scientific research—not simply on the word of God. These basic principles structure and limit the terms of our social debate. For example, a devout Catholic who opposes abortion cannot simply argue in a public debate that abortion is wrong because God says so. There is no way to argue with such a pronouncement, and it is not grounded in any social principles. Instead, the Catholic must argue against the legalization of abortion in secular terms by discussing the rights of the unborn and the sanctity of human life. She must give socially grounded arguments that can be addressed and challenged on their own terms.

One real danger with perfectionism is that it will translate into a kind of fundamentalism where individuals hold particular beliefs grounded in absolute rules of right or wrong for which no reasons are given and with which disagreement is not possible. An inclusion of perfectionist values in public debate need not, however, lead to such a clash of absolutes. Perfectionism can be placed within and be limited by the liberal frameworks we have already established. Liberal ideals can still define the boundaries of any discussion about how individuals should live and how society should be structured. For example, taking liberal rights as a starting point means that slavery on the basis of race or sex cannot be advocated as a legitimate ideal. Liberalism takes slavery out of the debate. Moreover, we can still demand that even perfectionist principles be defended in secular terms through logic and evidence and not simply through attribution to some higher truth.

Perfectionism is already deeply entrenched in the feminist debates permeating society. Despite most feminists' vociferous denials of an endorsement of a substantive conception of the good life, most women feel judged by such a standard. Moreover, feminists' criticisms are perfectionist because they have to be. Liberalism has achieved great strides for women, but the final frontier for feminism is in changing how women think about themselves and their lives. These changes cannot be argued for or justified in liberal terms. Feminism needs, despite the risks, to move beyond liberalism to a more open advocacy of the perfectionism it already endorses. If the values and arguments are strong, as I believe they are, then an open rather than hidden perfectionism has the potential for improving the quality of women's lives in the next millennium.

Notes

1. Introduction

1. A neutral principle is one that does not encourage or favor any particular way of life. As is discussed later, liberalism endorses neutral principles about how society should be structured but shuns perfectionist principles dictating how individuals should live.

2. For a discussion of the different number of hours women and men spend in paid employment see Victor R. Fuchs, *Women's Quest for Economic Equality* (Cambridge: Harvard University Press, 1988), p. 45. See also Barbara R. Bergmann, *The Economic Emergence of Women* (New York: Basic Books, 1986), table 11.2, p. 263. From the 1960s to the 1980s women working full-time year-round earned approximately 60 percent of what men working full-time year-round earned. This ratio improved during the 1980s, and by 1990 full-time working women earned approximately 72 percent of their male counterparts. See June O'Neill and Solomon Polachek, "Why the Gender Gap in Wages Narrowed in the 1980s," *Journal of Labor Economics* 11, no. 1 (1993): 205–206. By 1999, full-time working women earned approximately 77 percent of what full-time working men earned. See U.S. Census Bureau, *Statistical Abstract of the United States: 2000* (Washington, D.C.: Government Printing Office, 2000), table 696.

3. For numerous examples of such discrimination, see generally Susan Faludi, *Backlash: The Undeclared War against American Women* (New York: Crown Publishers, 1991).

4. I am not claiming that women and men are making different choices under exactly the same set of social pressures and expectations. Of course they are not. All decisions are made in a context of competing concerns, expectations, and potential repercussions. Contextual variance, however, does not render women's and men's decisions nonchoices; it simply helps explain why their choices differ so systematically.

5. *Statistical Abstract of the United States: 2000* (Washington, D.C.: General Printing Office, 2000), table 320. Likewise, 12 percent of the women and 5 percent of the men receiving bachelor's degrees in 1997 majored in education, while 12 percent of the men and 2 percent of the women receiving bachelor's degrees in 1997 majored in engineering. See Thomas D. Snyder, *Digest of Education Statistics, 2000* (Washington, D.C.: Government Printing Office, 2001), table 257 (online at http://nces.ed.gov/pubs2001/digest/introduction.html).

6. Fuchs, *Women's Quest for Economic Equality,* p. 61.

7. Fuchs, *Women's Quest for Economic Equality,* p. 47.

8. *Statistical Abstract of the United States: 1995* (Washington, D.C.: Government Printing Office, September 1995), table 636. I have rounded off percentages from this table.

9. Calculated from *Statistical Abstract of the United States: 1995,* tables 14 and 677.

10. *Statistical Abstract of the United States: 1995,* table 648. These numbers remain generally consistent with those analyzed by Fuchs. In 1986 only 7 percent of employed men between the ages of twenty-five and sixty-four worked fewer than thirty hours per week, compared with 21 percent of employed women. Married women and women with a child under six years of age were even more likely to work part-time. According to Fuchs, the fact that married white women are far more likely than married black women to work part-time suggests that such part-time status reflects the white women's life choices rather than their inability to find full-time work. See Fuchs, *Women's Quest for Economic Equality,* pp. 45–46.

11. Solomon W. Polachek and Charng Kao, "Lifetime Work Expectations and Estimates of Gender Discrimination," in *New Approaches to Economic and Social Analyses of Discrimination,* ed. Richard R. Cornwall and Phanindra V. Wunnava (New York: Praeger Publishers, 1991), p. 200.

12. More than twice as many women as men leave the labor force each year. O'Neill and Polachek, "Why the Gender Gap in Wages Narrowed in the 1980s," p. 219.

13. Randall K. Filer, "Male-Female Wage Differences: The Importance of Compensating Differentials," *Industrial and Labor Relations Review* 38, no. 3 (1985): 427.

14. Filer, "Male-Female Wage Differences," p. 428.

15. "Stanford Graduate School of Business Class of 1982," unpublished survey by Kaufman Associates (Menlo Park, Calif.), 1992.

16. These four occupations alone account for 13 percent of employed women. Calculated from *Statistical Abstract of the United States: 1995,* table 649.

17. These six occupations account for 17 percent of employed men (*Statistical Abstract of the United States: 1995,* table 649). These statistics suggest that not so much has changed since Fuchs calculated, using data from the 1980 census, that more than half of all female or male workers would have to change occupations in order for women and men to have the same job distribution. Fuchs, *Women's Quest for Economic Equality,* p. 33.

18. I assess only feminists' individually based choice critiques. These are arguments criticizing a choice because of the way the choice was made or because of the likely result of the choice to the decision maker. I do not assess feminist choice critiques that are grounded in a conception of group rights: arguments challenging particular individual choices not because of what they do to individuals but because of what they do to socially salient groups such as women or men. My focus is such because in a liberal democracy, feminists are far more likely to level, and find success with, individualistic rather than group-based arguments. This focus is also pragmatic. The two types of arguments are sufficiently different that an adequate discussion of the latter would require

a second book. For an example of a group-based argument regarding the harm of prostitution, see Debra Satz, "Markets in Women's Sexual Labor," *Ethics* 106 (October 1995): 63–85. Satz argues that the primary harm of prostitution is that, in the cultural context in which prostitution currently exists, it reinforces and "embodies an idea of women as inferior" (p. 78).

19.   I include autonomy on this list despite the debate between comprehensive and political liberals about whether or not liberalism calls for the promotion of autonomy because even if there is controversy about the extent to which the state must promote individual autonomy, the protection of individual autonomy is clearly a basic tenet of the liberal state.

20.   William A. Galston, *Liberal Purposes: Goods, Virtues, and Diversity in the Liberal State* (New York: Cambridge University Press, 1991), pp. 143–44. I actually believe not only that supposedly liberal rights are actually grounded in perfectionism but that liberal rights are employed in a distinctly perfectionist manner. In many cases where the state takes action to protect a liberal right, there are in fact several rights at stake and in conflict. The state's decision of which and whose right to protect reflects the state's hierarchy of the importance of the rights in particular instances. For the purposes of this book, however, I simply accept that there is a set of liberal rights that can be relied upon without relying on perfectionism.

INTRODUCTION TO PART I

1.   The term "sex worker" refers to women engaged in the explicit commodification and sale of their sexuality either through prostitution or through activities such as stripping or performing in pornography. I use the shorthand term "sex kittens" to refer to women who objectify their sexuality and conceive of their self-worth primarily in terms of their value as sex and beauty objects for men.

2. Three Hard Choices

1.   Despite the chasm that is often present between activists and academic theorists, I focus on the views of both because the opinions and activities of both groups shape society's general opinion about what "the feminist movement" stands for. To the extent that this book hopes to challenge the strength and sincerity of many viewpoints commonly understood to be feminist, it seems important to not limit my analysis to only those views expressed in scholarly feminist articles. Particularly in the discussion of sex work, I discuss the viewpoints expressed by women in the industry themselves. Some of the women cited may not identify themselves publicly as feminists, but they all see themselves as fighting for women's rights and gender equality. Furthermore, because women in the sex industry have been the most vocal supporters of women's choice to commodify their sexuality, feminist scholars are often in the position of challenging sexual commodification despite sex workers' own arguments in favor of the choice. It is this conflict between feminist scholars and pro-sex-

work activists that decidedly increases the problematic nature of the sex-work choice for feminists.

2. Off the continuum are the far more rare openly perfectionist arguments that focus not on the autonomy of the choice maker but on the nature of the choice. It is these arguments, I argue in later chapters, that provide the strongest justification for criticizing these choices.

3. For more on the differences between decriminalization and legalization see generally Gail Pheterson, ed., *A Vindication of the Rights of Whores* (Seattle: Seal Press, 1989).

4. See generally Frédérique Delacoste and Priscilla Alexander, eds., *Sex Work: Writings by Women in the Sex Industry* (Pittsburgh: Cleis Press, 1987); Pheterson, *A Vindication of the Rights of Whores;* Laurie Bell, ed., *Good Girls/Bad Girls: Feminists and Sex Trade Workers Face to Face* (Seattle: Seal Press, 1987).

5. "Coyote/National Task Force on Prostitution," in Delacoste and Alexander, eds., *Sex Work*, pp. 290–91.

6. Bell, *Good Girls/Bad Girls*, pp. 117–18. Mary Johnson was a participant at the 1985 conference in Toronto "Challenging Our Images: The Politics of Pornography and Prostitution," of which *Good Girls/Bad Girls* is a partial transcription.

7. See Priscilla Alexander, "Prostitution: A Difficult Issue for Feminists," in Delacoste and Alexander, eds., *Sex Work*, pp. 199–200.

8. Alexander, "Prostitution: A Difficult Issue for Feminists," pp. 199–200.

9. Alexander, "Prostitution: A Difficult Issue for Feminists," p. 200.

10. Alexander, "Prostitution: A Difficult Issue for Feminists," pp. 199–200.

11. Peggy Morgan, "Living on the Edge," in Delacoste and Alexander, eds., *Sex Work*, p. 25.

12. See, e.g., Martha C. Nussbaum, *Sex and Social Justice* (Oxford: Oxford University Press, 1999), chapter 11 (arguing that women's choice to engage in prostitution is made under the same limiting conditions that poor women make other life choices and that the choice to prostitute oneself is not more inherently oppressive than other forms of labor).

13. Pheterson, *A Vindication of the Rights of Whores*, p. 146.

14. Morgan, "Living on the Edge," p. 25. Generally the argument that sex work is just like other kinds of work is a fairly mild and neutral claim. The argument is that sex work is no more incompatible with human fulfillment and a good human life than are many other forms of work. Usually, though, feminists who respect women's choice to become sex workers do not go so far as to argue that sex work is affirmatively a good type of work, one that promotes human flourishing. The claims are usually that it is at most neutral; neither is it demeaning nor does it enhance the quality of one's life.

Some who think that sex work is a legitimate choice for women do, however, make the more affirmative claim that sex work is a valuable career choice that should actually be encouraged and not merely tolerated. The argument suggests a kind of pro-sex-work perfectionism. Sex work can actually promote human flourishing. The Canadian Organization for the Rights of Prostitutes (CORP) reflects this view when in response to the question "Is prostitution a good in and of itself?" it answers: "'Of course it is. . . . Anonymous sex is as valid as any other kind of sex." Bell, *Good Girls/Bad Girls*, p. 208. The strongest statement about the value to the individual of sex work itself that I have seen was made by Valerie Scott, a participant at the 1985 "Challenging Our Images" conference. Scott equates the value and worth of sex work with that of musical or athletic activity. Scott challenges: "If your daughter or son showed tendencies toward ballet or piano, you would encourage them probably. Now if they showed tendencies toward prostitution, would you encourage them? My suggestion is, find out what the business is about and inform them. And if they choose to go that route, help them. . . . " (Bell, *Good Girls/Bad Girls*, p. 123).

My guess is that even most people who respect women's choices to commodify their sexuality would feel uncomfortable putting the choice on par with the development of one's musical or athletic talents. Most people probably do not feel comfortable encouraging sex work as a positive and fulfilling life choice for girls and boys. This argument seems to be extreme even among those who think sex work is a socially legitimate and acceptable choice. Arguments about the value of prostituting oneself are relied on much less frequently than are the more standard pro-prostitution autonomy-based arguments that remain comfortably agnostic on the value of the work itself.

15. Bell, *Good Girls/Bad Girls*, pp. 48–49.

16. Catharine A. MacKinnon, "Prostitution and Civil Rights," *Michigan Journal of Gender & Law* 1 (1993): 13, 25–26. See also Dorchen Leidholdt, "Prostitution: A Violation of Women's Human Rights," *Cardozo Women's Law Journal* 1 (1993): 133 (arguing that women who enter prostitution are often violently forced to remain in the industry).

17. MacKinnon, "Prostitution and Civil Rights," pp. 24–26.

18. Margaret A. Baldwin, "Strategies of Connection: Prostitution and Feminist Politics," *Michigan Journal of Gender & Law* 1 (1993): 71. See also Kathleen Barry, *Female Sexual Slavery* (New York: New York University Press, 1979); Nancy Erbe, "Prostitutes: Victims of Men's Exploitation and Abuse," *Journal of Law & Inequality* 2 (1984): 611.

19. Sarah Wynter, "Whisper: Women Hurt in Systems of Prostitution Engaged in Revolt," in Delacoste and Alexander, eds., *Sex Work*, p. 267.

20. Susan Kay Hunter, "Prostitution Is Cruelty and Abuse to Women and Children," *Michigan Journal of Gender & Law* 1 (1993): 95.

21. Wynter, "Whisper," p. 268.

22. Wynter, "Whisper," pp. 268–69. See also Christine Overall, "What's Wrong with Prostitution? Evaluating Sex Work," *Signs: Journal of Women in Culture and Society* 17 (1992): 711.

23. MacKinnon, "Prostitution and Civil Rights," p. 26. Presumably the coercion that MacKinnon refers to here is the more standard version of threatened rights violations.

24. Catharine A. MacKinnon, *Feminism Unmodified: Discourses on Life and Law* (Cambridge: Harvard University Press, 1987), p. 180.

25. Morgan, "Living on the Edge," p. 24.

26. See Alexander, "Prostitution: A Difficult Issue for Feminists," p. 188.

27. Catharine A. MacKinnon, *Toward a Feminist Theory of the State* (Cambridge: Harvard University Press, 1989), p. 147.

28. MacKinnon, "Prostitution and Civil Rights," pp. 27–28. For other accounts of this view see Dorchen Leidholdt, "Prostitution: A Violation of Women's Human Rights," p. 133; Susan Kay Hunter, "Prostitution Is Cruelty and Abuse to Women and Children," p. 91.

29. Wynter, "Whisper," p. 268.

30. Catharine A. MacKinnon, "Feminism, Marxism, Method and the State: An Agenda for Theory," *Signs* 7 (1982): 515, 534. See also Catharine A. MacKinnon, "Feminism, Marxism, Method and the State: Toward Feminist Jurisprudence," *Signs* 8 (1983): 635, and MacKinnon, *Toward a Feminist Theory of the State*.

31. MacKinnon, "Prostitution and Civil Rights," p. 28. Debra Satz extends this argument. She suggests that prostitution is problematic not only because it arises out of conditions of social gender inequality but also because the practice reinforces these patterns of sex discrimination and inequality. See Debra Satz, "Markets in Women's Sexual Labor," *Ethics* 106 (October 1995): 63.

32. Wynter, "Whisper," p. 269.

33. Wynter, "Whisper," p. 269.

34. Hunter, "Prostitution Is Cruelty and Abuse to Women and Children," p. 96.

35. MacKinnon, "Prostitution and Civil Rights," p. 25. See also Barry, *Female Sexual Slavery;* Leidholdt, "Prostitution: A Violation of Women's Human Rights." The Council for Prostitution Alternatives documented the crimes committed against a sample of prostitutes by their pimps and johns. Seventy-eight percent were victims of rape, usually multiple rapes; 84 percent were victims of aggravated assault; 49 percent were victims of kidnapping; 53 percent were victims of sexual abuse through torture. Hunter, "Prostitution Is Cruelty and Abuse to Women and Children," pp. 92–94.

36. Erbe, "Prostitutes: Victims of Men's Exploitation and Abuse," pp. 609, 611–12. According to Erbe, "pimps control prostitutes through 1) physical abuse; 2) physical control of prostitutes' children . . . ; 3) serious threats of physical harm . . . ; 4) keeping prostitutes in continuous states of poverty and indebtedness; and 5) ensuring that prostitutes have no freedom to move outside unaccompanied" (pp. 612–13).

There is also a far less common perfectionist argument against sex work that parallels the perfectionist argument in support of it. The anti-sex-work perfectionist argument claims that there is something special about sex work that makes it different from other kinds of work and that makes it more degrading to personhood than other forms of work. Even if sex work is freely chosen, the choice should be considered illegitimate because it harms the individual involved, and others, by demeaning and damaging their value as human beings. Andrea Dworkin makes this argument in its purest form. Prostitution in all its forms degrades the individual and destroys one's personhood. The practice necessarily changes a person into an object. See Andrea Dworkin, "Prostitution and Male Supremacy," *Michigan Journal of Gender & Law* 1 (1993): 2–3. Carole Pateman argues that sex work degrades women because it involves the purchase and direct use of a woman's body rather than the purchase of her services, as is the case in other jobs. See Carole Pateman, "Defending Prostitution: Charges against Ericsson," *Ethics* 93 (1983): 562; Carole Pateman, *The Sexual Contract* (Stanford, Calif.: Stanford University Press, 1988), p. 207. See also Erbe, "Prostitutes: Victims of Men's Exploitation and Abuse," p. 623 (arguing that prostitution leads to "guilt, self-disgust, and a learned sense of worthlessness" for the women involved). Elizabeth Anderson argues that prostitution degrades both the women participating in the sex industry and all women by making it difficult for women to conceive of and treat their sexuality as an integral and noncommodifiable part of their personhood. See Elizabeth Anderson, *Value in Ethics and Economics* (Cambridge: Harvard University Press, 1993), p. 155.

37.   Karen Lehrman, *The Lipstick Proviso: Women, Sex and Power in the Real World* (New York: Doubleday, 1997), p. 171, 173–74.

38.   Lehrman, *The Lipstick Proviso*, p. 69.

39.   Lehrman, *The Lipstick Proviso*, p. 82.

40.   Given the ambiguous nature of sexual objectification and the fact that objectification is largely in the eye of the beholder, the debate over women's decisions to objectify their sexuality for men may not look like a debate at all. It may look like the two sides are discussing totally different behaviors. The sides are not disagreeing in their assessment of the same activity but are instead reaching different conclusions about different activities. This is to some extent true and to some extent an illusion. Feminists who think women's choices to sexually objectify themselves are legitimate and feminists who think such choices are not legitimate seem to be talking about different choices because choices are characterized differently depending upon the side doing the talking. Feminists challenging the legitimacy of women's choices to sexually objectify themselves normally characterize the choices as arising under conditions in which women's choices are severely constrained.

41.   Naomi Wolf, *The Beauty Myth: How Images of Beauty Are Used against Women* (New York: William Morrow and Company, 1991), pp. 258–59.

42.   Wolf, *The Beauty Myth*, p. 258.

43.   The mechanism through which women internalize the messages of pornography and sexual violence such that they sexualize themselves and their subordination is not clear. The mechanism seems to be less one of women's conscious adoption of the messages and norms put forth in pornography and more of an

unconscious absorption of the roles and sexual ideology that pornography and systemic sexual violence suggest.

44. MacKinnon, *Feminism Unmodified,* pp. 53–54.

45. MacKinnon, *Toward a Feminist Theory of the State,* p. 149.

46. Rita Freedman, *Beauty Bound: Why We Pursue the Myth in the Mirror* (Lexington, Mass.: Lexington Books, 1986), p. 37.

47. Freedman, *Beauty Bound,* p. 25.

48. Freedman, *Beauty Bound,* pp. 32–35. Related to the vulnerability argument is the more openly perfectionist argument that the choice to self-objectify demeans and degrades a person's self-esteem and value regardless of whether or not the woman comes at some later point in life to regret the decision. The perfectionist argument challenging the legitimacy of women's choices to sexually objectify themselves argues simply that conceiving of one's self largely or entirely as an object for others' pleasure and enjoyment, particularly as an object for others' aesthetic and sexual pleasure and enjoyment, is both literally and actually dehumanizing. Self-objectification is incompatible with a meaningful human life precisely because it denies one's humanity—one's capacity and need for intellectual and creative stimulation—as well as one's individuality. Self-objectification means that one exists for and is valued exclusively by others; such object status is incompatible with the self-love and self-respect necessary for a meaningful human life. Freedman makes this feminist perfectionist argument against women's self-objectification. "Objectification changes body image and erodes self-esteem. To be objectified means to be seen as a thing that exists for the viewer. As object rather than subject, a woman suffers a kind of 'psychic annihilation.' As object, her existence depends on the observer, who can either bring her to life by recognizing her or snuff her out by ignoring her" (Freedman, *Beauty Bound,* p. 37). Self-objectification seems incompatible not only with a fulfilling human life but perhaps with any independent and self-sustaining human life at all.

49. Lehrman, *The Lipstick Proviso,* p. 138.

50. Reva Landau, "On Making 'Choices,'" *Feminist Issues* (1992): 62.

51. Joan C. Williams, "Deconstructing Gender," *Michigan Law Review* 87 (1989): 829.

52. Kathleen Gerson, *Hard Choices* (Berkeley: University of California Press, 1985), pp. 136–38.

53. Susan Okin, *Justice, Gender, and the Family* (New York: Basic Books, 1989), p. 143.

54. Okin, *Justice, Gender, and the Family,* p. 148.

55. Okin, *Justice, Gender, and the Family,* p. 148.

56. Okin, *Justice, Gender, and the Family,* p. 147.

57. Okin, *Justice, Gender, and the Family,* p. 147.

58. Okin, *Justice, Gender, and the Family,* pp. 143–44.

59. Okin, *Justice, Gender, and the Family,* p. 144.

60. Okin, *Justice, Gender, and the Family,* p. 142.

61. Williams, "Deconstructing Gender," p. 831.

62. Landau, "On Making 'Choices,'" p. 56.

63. Williams, "Deconstructing Gender," p. 833.

64. Williams, "Deconstructing Gender," p. 824.

65. Williams, "Deconstructing Gender," p. 824.

66. Landau, "On Making 'Choices,'" pp. 47–48. Feminists also criticize women's choices to be full-time homemakers because the choices make women vulnerable in noneconomic ways. For example, Okin criticizes the homemaker choice because it constrains women's future options. See Okin, *Justice, Gender, and the Family,* p. 151. Margaret Baldwin criticizes the choice because women's economic dependence on their husbands results in a loss of self-respect and a psychological dependence on their economic providers. Margaret A. Baldwin, "Public Women and the Feminist State," *Harvard Women's Law Journal* 20 (1997): 83. These vulnerability arguments—focusing on women's loss of future options and loss of self-esteem—are more directly perfectionist than are the arguments focusing on women's loss of income and wealth. Their focus is not on ensuring fair and free conditions for choice but on ensuring that women possess particular options and particular types of self-esteem because these things are essential for human flourishing.

3. An Introduction to Perfectionism

1. Thomas Hurka, *Perfectionism* (Oxford: Oxford University Press, 1993), p. 3.

2. See Vinit Haksar, *Equality, Liberty, and Perfectionism* (Oxford: Oxford University Press, 1977), pp. 3–4. Of the writers discussed in the current chapter, Joseph Raz presents a version of intrinsic perfectionism while Thomas Hurka, George Sher, and Martha Nussbaum all present inherent perfectionisms.

3. Joseph Raz, *The Morality of Freedom* (Oxford: Clarendon Press, 1990), p. 7.

4. Raz, *The Morality of Freedom,* pp. 6–7.

5. Although, as will be seen shortly, the only autonomy that Raz truly finds intrinsically valuable is that directed at valuable or good ends.

6. Raz, *The Morality of Freedom,* pp. 372–73.

7. Raz, *The Morality of Freedom,* pp. 373–75, 378. A "person must have options which enable him to sustain throughout his life activities which, taken together, exercise all the capacities human beings have an innate drive to exercise, as well as to decline to develop any of them" (p. 375).

8. Raz, *The Morality of Freedom,* pp. 381, 412.

9. Raz, *The Morality of Freedom,* p. 348.

10. Raz, *The Morality of Freedom,* pp. 347–53.

11. Raz, *The Morality of Freedom,* p. 352.

12.   Raz, *The Morality of Freedom*, p. 353.

13.   See Raz, *The Morality of Freedom*, p. 161.

14.   Raz, *The Morality of Freedom*, pp. 1–2.

15.   Raz, *The Morality of Freedom*, p. 418.

16.   Raz, *The Morality of Freedom*, p. 161. Raz continues: "[S]upporting valuable forms of life is a social rather than an individual matter. Monogamy, assuming that it is the only morally valuable form of marriage, cannot be practised by an individual. It requires a culture which recognizes it, and which supports it through the public's attitude and through its formal institutions" (p. 162).

17.   See generally John Stuart Mill, *On Liberty*, ed. Alburey Castell (Wheeling, Ill.: Harlan Davidson, 1947).

18.   Raz, *The Morality of Freedom*, p. 416.

19.   Raz, *The Morality of Freedom*, p. 417.

20.   Raz, *The Morality of Freedom*, p. 417.

21.   Raz, *The Morality of Freedom*, p. 381. Raz claims to focus on the intrinsic value of autonomy, but his claims that only valuable autonomy is important for human flourishing seem inexorably tied to a conception of the inherent goodness of particular activities for a good human life.

22.   Hurka, *Perfectionism*, p. 3.

23.   Hurka, *Perfectionism*, pp. 10–11.

24.   Hurka, *Perfectionism*, pp. 11–12.

25.   Hurka, *Perfectionism*, p. 16.

26.   Hurka, *Perfectionism*, p. 17.

27.   Hurka, *Perfectionism*, pp. 39–40.

28.   Hurka, *Perfectionism*, p. 37.

29.   Hurka, *Perfectionism*, p. 38.

30.   Hurka, *Perfectionism*, p. 39.

31.   Hurka, *Perfectionism*, p. 41.

32.   Hurka, *Perfectionism*, p. 158.

33.   Hurka, *Perfectionism*, pp. 31–32. There does, however, seem to be some tension in Hurka's theory and some suggestion that he may not really be entirely amoral in its application. For example, Hurka rejected the equation of human nature with those characteristics that are distinctive of humans because he argued that certain characteristics distinctive to humans are also repulsive, such as killing for fun. See Hurka, *Perfectionism*, pp. 10–11. It is, however, difficult to reject a conception of human nature on the grounds that certain activities are repulsive and not worthy of development without having an implicit moral compass in one's conception of the good life.

34.   Hurka, *Perfectionism*, p. 20.

35.   Hurka, *Perfectionism*, pp. 147, 159.

36. Hurka, *Perfectionism,* p. 159.

37. Hurka, *Perfectionism,* p. 159.

38. Sher, *Beyond Neutrality,* p. 246.

39. Sher, *Beyond Neutrality,* p. 11.

40. Sher, *Beyond Neutrality,* p. 246.

41. Sher, *Beyond Neutrality,* p. 246.

42. Sher, *Beyond Neutrality,* p. 202.

43. Sher, *Beyond Neutrality,* p. 229.

44. Sher, *Beyond Neutrality,* pp. 203–206.

45. Sher, *Beyond Neutrality,* pp. 203–206.

46. Sher, *Beyond Neutrality,* p. 203.

47. Sher, *Beyond Neutrality,* p. 203.

48. Sher, *Beyond Neutrality,* p. 203.

49. Sher, *Beyond Neutrality,* p. 203.

50. Sher, *Beyond Neutrality,* p. 204. The universality or unavoidability of Sher's rational activity seems to be called into question by the not uncommon attempts by people to effectively abandon their autonomy and cede control over their lives to someone or something else. For a discussion of this impulse see generally Robin West, "Authority, Autonomy, and Choice: The Role of Consent in the Moral and Political Visions of Franz Kafka and Richard Posner," *Harvard Law Review* 99 (1985): 384.

51. Sher, *Beyond Neutrality,* p. 205.

52. Sher, *Beyond Neutrality,* p. 204.

53. Sher, *Beyond Neutrality,* p. 204.

54. Sher, *Beyond Neutrality,* pp. 205–206.

55. Sher, *Beyond Neutrality,* p. 206.

56. Sher, *Beyond Neutrality,* p. 208.

57. Sher, *Beyond Neutrality,* pp. 205–207.

58. Sher, *Beyond Neutrality,* p. 208.

59. Sher, *Beyond Neutrality,* pp. 208–13.

60. Sher, *Beyond Neutrality,* p. 208.

61. Sher, *Beyond Neutrality,* p. 208.

62. Sher, *Beyond Neutrality,* p. 208.

63. Sher, *Beyond Neutrality,* p. 208.

64. Sher, *Beyond Neutrality,* p. 209. It is unclear on what Sher grounds his assertion that moral reasons are often the best reasons on which to act. It seems that this should only be the case if the goal of one's actions is itself moral in nature. One could, however, act completely reasonably toward a goal that is either amoral or immoral. As Hurka suggests, the fundamental capacity of practical rationality

need not be exercised with morality as a constituent goal, in which case the morality of the reasons one considers would be irrelevant.

65. Sher, *Beyond Neutrality,* p. 209.

66. Sher, *Beyond Neutrality,* p. 213.

67. Sher only suggests one relationship that clearly fails to provide adequate mutual recognition: this is the master-slave relationship. Sher, *Beyond Neutrality,* pp. 206–207.

68. Raz indicates as much when he says autonomy requires that an adequate range of options be available to the individual. Raz, *The Morality of Freedom,* p. 373.

69. Jeremy Waldron, "Autonomy and Perfectionism in Raz's Morality of Freedom," *Southern California Law Review* 62 (1989): 1097, 1129.

70. Waldron, "Autonomy and Perfectionism," p. 1130.

71. Nussbaum does not specify if any causal link is required between an individual's deprivation and the choices she makes in order to justify challenging the choices. It is imaginable that a woman could make a choice under conditions of deprivation, according to Nussbaum's list, but for reasons unrelated to her deprivation. For example, a poor woman might choose to act as a surrogate mother for a middle-class couple who will pay for her services. But she may choose to do so because she wants to bring another being in the world and give other individuals the opportunity for parenthood they might not otherwise have, not because she is impoverished.

72. Nussbaum's list typically includes all of the following:

1. Being able to live to the end of a normal human life.

2. Being able to have good health, adequate nourishment and shelter, opportunities for sexual satisfaction, choice in matters of reproduction, and geographic mobility.

3. Being able to avoid unnecessary pain and to have pleasure.

4. Being able to use the senses, to imagine, to think, and to reason and doing these things in a way cultivated and informed by education.

5. Being able to have attachments to things and persons outside oneself.

6. Being able to form a conception of the good and a plan of one's own life. This includes being able to work in the public sphere and to participate in political life.

7. Being able to engage in various forms of social interaction; having the capability for justice, friendship, compassion, and empathy.

8. Being able to live with and have concern for animals, plants, and the world of nature.

9. Being able to laugh, play, and recreate.

10. Being able to live one's life and make life choices without undue interference, especially with respect to personal and self-defining choices such as those regarding marriage, childbearing, sexual expression, speech, and employment.

This list is a shortened version of the one appearing in Martha C. Nussbaum, "Human Capabilities, Female Human Beings," in *Women, Culture, and Development: A Study of Human Capabilities,* ed. Martha Nussbaum and Jonathan Glover (Oxford: Clarendon Press, 1995), pp. 83–85.

73.   Martha Nussbaum, "Nature, Function, and Capability: Aristotle on Political Distribution," *Oxford Studies in Ancient Philosophy,* suppl. vol. 1 (1988): 160.

74.   Nussbaum, "Nature, Function, and Capability," p. 161.

75.   Nussbaum, "Nature, Function, and Capability," pp. 163–64.

76.   Nussbaum, "Nature, Function, and Capability," p. 164.

77.   Nussbaum, "Human Capabilities," pp. 94–95.

78.   See Nussbaum's response to the liberal challenges of her own theory on the grounds that she does not adequately respect individual autonomy. She states that "a respect for choice is built deeply into the list itself" and is adamant that her capability approach does not require any particular choice outcomes. Nussbaum, "Human Capabilities," pp. 94–95.

79.   Nussbaum, "Human Capabilities," pp. 94–95.

80.   Nussbaum, "Human Capabilities," p. 95.

81.   Martha C. Nussbaum, "Human Functioning and Social Justice: In Defense of Aristotelian Essentialism," *Political Theory* 20, no. 2 (May 1992): 235.

82.   Nussbaum, "Human Functioning and Social Justice," pp. 203, 234.

83.   Martha Chen, *A Quiet Revolution: Women in Transition in Rural Bangladesh* (Cambridge, Mass.: Schenkman, 1983). See also Martha Chen, "A Matter of Survival: Women's Right to Employment in India and Bangladesh," in Nussbaum and Glover, eds., *Women, Culture, and Development: A Study of Human Capabilities.*

84.   Nussbaum, "Human Functioning and Social Justice," p. 235.

85.   Nussbaum, "Human Functioning and Social Justice," pp. 235–36.

86.   Nussbaum, "Human Functioning and Social Justice," pp. 236–37.

87.   Obviously not all schools help children develop even these basic capabilities. See Jonathan Kozol, *Savage Inequalities: Children in America's Schools* (New York: HarperCollins, 1992). It is important, though, that girls are no more likely than are boys to attend inadequate schools. Hence, both girls and boys are equally likely to develop the required capabilities.

88.   All states provide some economic safety net in the form of public assistance, soup kitchens, and homeless shelters. Similarly, a right to education, at least through high school, and a right to determine one's own life path, at least in adulthood, are also guaranteed by law. Of course, these formal guarantees do not mean that some people are indeed without food, housing, education, and control over their lives.

89.   In fact, women's educational attainment at these levels has surpassed men's. In 1994, among persons 16 to 24 years old, 12.3 percent of the men were high school dropouts as opposed to 8.1 percent of the women. More women

than men also enrolled in college. In 1994, 60.6 percent of male high school graduates enrolled in college, as opposed to 63.2 percent of female high school graduates. In absolute terms more women than men are also earning bachelor's degrees. In 1992–93, 532,881 men earned their bachelor's degrees as opposed to 632,297 women. See Thomas D. Snyder and Charlene M. Hoffman, *Digest of Education Statistics 1995* (Washington, D.C.: Government Printing Office, 1995), pp. 110, 188, 250.

4. Coercion Critiques

1. The key to coercion critiques, and the factor that I consider to be the distinguishing one between choices resulting from coercion and those resulting from socialization, which I discuss in the next chapter, is that a woman whose choice is coerced knows that she is choosing an option that is not her first choice in order to avoid a consequence which she dislikes even more. A woman whose choice is the product of socialization is choosing her most preferred option even if we have reason to criticize her preference ordering.

2. In robbery and extortion the individual's submission to violence or threatened violence is considered invalid. The difference between the two crimes depends on whether the victim gave consent, albeit coerced consent, to the theft of property, or whether property was just taken by force. According to California Penal Code Section 211: "Robbery is the felonious taking of personal property in the possession of another, from his person or immediate presence, and against his will, accomplished by means of force or fear." According to California Penal Code Section 518: "Extortion is the obtaining of property from another, with his consent, or the obtaining of an official act of a public officer, induced by a wrongful use of force or fear, or under color of official right." For a case on the blurry line between robbery and extortion see *People v. Jacobsen*, 11 Cal. App. 2d 728 (1936).

   Rape law, too, invalidates a woman's "consent" to sex made in response to threats of violence. See *Commonwealth v. Williams*, 439 A.2d 765 (Pa. Super. 1982) (affirming rape conviction of defendant who threatened to kill his victim if she resisted; court held the woman's "consent" was not legitimate and did not negate the defendant's mens rea [criminal intent]); see also Stephen J. Schulhofer, *Unwanted Sex: The Culture of Intimidation and the Failure of Law* (Cambridge: Harvard University Press, 1998), p. 3.

3. See American Law Institute, *Model Penal Code*, official draft and explanatory notes (Philadelphia: American Law Institute, 1985). Duress "is an affirmative defense that the actor engaged in the conduct charged to constitute an offense because he was coerced to do so by the use of, or a threat to use, unlawful force against his person or the person of another, that a person of reasonable firmness in his situation would have been unable to resist." See also *United States v. Contento-Pachon*, 723 F.2d 691 (9th Cir. 1984) (defendant adequately raised defense of duress by showing he transported illegal drugs under an immediate and well-grounded threat of serious bodily injury).

4. Threats of economic injury as well as threats of bodily harm constitute duress sufficient to void a contract entered into under such conditions. See *Austin Instrument, Inc. v. Loral Corporation*, 272 N.E.2d 533 (N.Y. Ct. App. 1971) (contract terms voided because contract entered into under economic duress). The principle of unconscionability covers both unfairness in the bargaining process leading to the formation of the contract as well as unfairness in the terms of the contract itself. According to comment c to section 208 of the Restatement (Second) of Contracts, "Theoretically it is possible for a contract to be oppressive taken as a whole, even though there is no weakness in the bargaining process and no single term which is in itself unconscionable." See *Henningsen v. Bloomfield Motors, Inc.*, 161 A.2d 69 (N.J. S.Ct. 1969) (invalidating contract terms because of the unequal bargaining power of the parties and because the terms themselves contravened public policy).

5. The early common law recognized only four types of duress: (1) fear of loss of life; (2) fear of loss of limb; (3) fear of mayhem; and (4) fear of imprisonment. See Samuel Williston, *A Treatise on the Law of Contracts*, 3rd. ed. (Rochester, N.Y.: Baker, Voorhis & Co., the Lawyers Co-operative Publishing Co., 1970), section 1601, p. 649; James A. Harley, "Economic Duress and Unconscionability: How Fair Must the Government Be?" *Public Contract Law Journal* 18: 76, 80 (1988).

6. Toward the end of the nineteenth century, the law of duress began to expand to include agreements made in response to threats to one's property as well as to one's person. The Supreme Court in *French v. Shoemaker*, 81 U.S. (14 Wall.) 314 (1871) marked the early shift. According to the Court, "Decided cases may be found which deny that contracts procured by menace of a mere battery to the person or of trespass to lands, or of loss to goods, can be avoided on that account, . . . but the modern decisions in this country adopt a more liberal rule, and hold that contracts procured by threats of battery to the person or of destruction of property may be avoided on the ground of duress." 81 U.S. (14 Wall.) 314, 332 (1871).

7. Frequently, as in this case, coercion involves threats both to one's rights and to one's existing level of well-being.

8. Robert Nozick, "Coercion," in *Philosophy, Science, and Method*, ed. Sidney Morgenbesser et al. (New York: St. Martin's Press, 1969), p. 450.

9. This example is useful but inherently awkward since it is paradoxical to think about slaves having socially recognized liberal rights yet still being slaves.

10. Alan Wertheimer, *Coercion* (Princeton, N.J.: Princeton University Press, 1987), pp. 213–14.

11. This example is an adapted version of one Wertheimer presents. See Wertheimer, *Coercion*, p. 211.

12. The woman's decision, of course, could cause harm to third-party shopkeepers who might sell goods and services to the mugger before the woman cancels her credit cards.

13.   Clearly, one could argue that in neither scenario is Alex really facing a threatened rights violation because he has given up his right to liberty by breaking a community law, and therefore neither choice is really coerced.

14.   Often, as in this case, this version of coercion looks like a standard form of blackmail.

15.   Nozick, "Coercion," p. 450.

16.   Wertheimer, *Coercion*, pp. 213–14.

17.   John Stuart Mill, *Utilitarianism*, ed. Oskar Piest (New York: Macmillan, 1957), p. 66.

18.   Mill, *Utilitarianism*, p. 67.

19.   Part of Posner's criticism of utilitarianism is that it does not effectively protect individual rights because it does not differentiate between kinds of happiness and it permits the sacrifice of the one for the increased happiness of the group. Posner refers to this as the "moral monstrousness" of utilitarianism (Richard A. Posner, "Utilitarianism, Economics, and Legal Theory," *Journal of Legal Studies* 8 [1979]: 116). As Posner recognizes, not all utilitarianisms are equally susceptible to this criticism. Rule utilitarianism avoids the "sacrifice of the innocent for the happiness of the many" problem. John Stuart Mill's utilitarianism, by incorporating perfectionism, avoids the problem of endorsing asocial behavior by incorporating an appreciation of virtue into the individual's pleasure and pain calculations. According to Mill, in order to truly maximize social happiness, people must incorporate the will to be good and virtuous into their character such that they associate doing right with pleasure (Mill, *Utilitarianism*, p. 51).

20.   Posner, "Utilitarianism, Economics, and Legal Theory," p. 125. This is, essentially, a restatement of the Coase Theorem that if transactions are costless, the initial assignment of a property right will not affect the ultimate use of the property. See Ronald H. Coase, "The Problem of Social Cost," *Journal of Law & Economics* 3 (October 1960): 1–44.

21.   Posner, "Utilitarianism, Economics, and Legal Theory," p. 125.

22.   Posner, "Utilitarianism, Economics, and Legal Theory," p. 125. Posner's wealth-maximization justification for vesting and protecting individual rights relies on the same kind of fundamental yet unprovable assumption about what maximizes wealth, as opposed to happiness, as did the utilitarian justification for individual rights.

23.   Immanuel Kant, *Groundwork of the Metaphysic of Morals*, trans. H. J. Paton (New York: Harper & Row, 1956), p. 79.

24.   Kant, *Groundwork of the Metaphysic of Morals*, p. 88.

25.   Kant, *Groundwork of the Metaphysic of Morals*, p. 96.

26.   Kant, *Groundwork of the Metaphysics of Morals*, p. 96.

27.   Ronald Dworkin, *Taking Rights Seriously* (London: Gerald Duckworth & Co., 1977), pp. 272–73.

28. Dworkin, *Taking Rights Seriously*, pp. 272–73.

29. Dworkin, *Taking Rights Seriously*, pp. 273–74.

30. Edmund Burke, *Reflections on the French Revolution* (New York: Anchor Books, 1989), p. 109.

31. Burke, *Reflections on the French Revolution*, pp. 108–109.

32. Burke, *Reflections on the French Revolution*, pp. 108–109. For example, Burke vehemently criticized the leaders of the French Revolution for changing private property rights after the revolution. Burke argued: "Of what import is it, under what names you injure men, and deprive them of the just emoluments of a profession, in which they were not only permitted but encouraged by the state to engage; and upon the supposed certainty of which emoluments they had formed the plan of their lives, contracted debts, and led multitudes to an entire dependence upon them?" (p. 120).

33. Burke, *Reflections on the French Revolution*, p. 100.

34. The Supreme Court's stare decisis argument in *Planned Parenthood of Southeastern Pennsylvania v. Casey*, 505 U.S. 833 (1992), for retaining the essential right to an abortion guaranteed by *Roe v. Wade*, 410 U.S. 113 (1973), takes this form. According to the Court:

    > The *Roe* rule's limitation on state power could not be repudiated without serious inequity to people who, for two decades of economic and social developments, have organized intimate relationships and made choices that define their views of themselves and their places in society, in reliance on the availability of abortion in the event that contraception should fail. The ability of women to participate equally in the economic and social life of the Nation has been facilitated by their ability to control their reproductive lives. The Constitution serves human values, and while the effect of reliance on *Roe* cannot be exactly measured, neither can the certain costs of overruling *Roe* for people who have ordered their thinking and living around that case be dismissed.

    Casey, 505 U.S. at 856.

35. Fried's conventionalism differs from Burke's in that he gives a large role to the importance of philosophy in determining general social organization, whereas Burke does not give any such role to philosophy.

36. Charles Fried, "The Artificial Reason of the Law or: What Lawyers Know," *Texas Law Review* 60 (1981): 35–58.

37. Fried, "The Artificial Reason of the Law," p. 37.

38. Fried, "The Artificial Reason of the Law," p. 54.

39. Fried, "The Artificial Reason of the Law," p. 57.

40. Fried, "The Artificial Reason of the Law," p. 57.

41. The autonomy arguments described in this section promise less than the autonomy argument put forth by Joseph Raz. While Raz favors only autonomy

directed toward certain valuable pursuits—though, as discussed previously, he did not describe what those valuable pursuits are—the autonomy arguments described here advocate more neutral and substanceless versions of autonomy.

42. Compare comprehensive liberals' endorsement of autonomy (see Brian Barry, *Justice as Impartiality: A Treatise on Social Justice* [Oxford: Clarendon Press, 1995]; and Amy Gutmann, "Civil Education and Social Diversity," *Ethics* 105 [April 1995]: 557–579) with political liberals' rejection of autonomy as a liberal value (see William A. Galston, "Two Concepts of Liberalism," *Ethics* 105: 516; and John Rawls, *Political Liberalism* [New York: Columbia University Press, 1993]).

     Both Sher and Hurka also include an endorsement of autonomy in their perfectionist theories; however, like the liberals discussed here, they did not describe any required outward manifestations of autonomy. Their autonomy, like that of the liberals, remains neutral and substanceless. The perfectionist arguments I uncover within contemporary feminism and the perfectionism I advocate is far more substantive than the versions of neutral autonomy endorsed by these liberal and perfectionist theorists.

43. Ernest J. Weinrib, *The Idea of Private Law* (Cambridge: Harvard University Press, 1995), pp. 81–91.

44. Joel Feinberg, *Rights, Justice, and the Bounds of Liberty: Essays in Social Philosophy* (Princeton, N.J.: Princeton University Press, 1980), p. 20.

45. Cass R. Sunstein, *Free Markets and Social Justice* (Oxford: Oxford University Press, 1997), p. 62.

46. Barry, *Justice as Impartiality*, p. 129.

47. Gerald Dworkin, *The Theory and Practice of Autonomy* (Cambridge: Cambridge University Press, 1988), p. 155.

48. Dworkin, *The Theory and Practice of Autonomy*, p. 155.

49. Dworkin, *The Theory and Practice of Autonomy*, p. 155.

50. Dworkin's justifications do not, however, explain why an endorsement of autonomy does not also lead to the invalidation of many other choices society considers legitimate and binding. For example, if a loss of autonomy is defined as the substitution of another's will for that of the individual decision maker, then it is hard to distinguish what is problematic about threatened rights violations from what is problematic about any other choice made because of someone else's influence. How can we distinguish between what is problematic about "Do X, or I'll kill you," which involves a clear rights violation, and "Do X, or I'll behave contemptuously toward you," which clearly does not? In both cases the individual performs X only because some other individual wills that she does. It would, however, be a very expansive and socially meaningless conception of autonomy to argue that a person's autonomy is intact only when everyone else is indifferent to her choice and thereby exercises no influence over it.

     Similarly, if autonomy is defined as having unconstrained choices, then why do some constraints seem more problematic for autonomy than others? Why does the constraint "If you do X, I will kill you" seem to be more of an infringement on autonomy than does the constraint "You cannot afford to do X." It may be because the first condition is a constraint on negative liberty while the second condition is a restraint on positive liberty. It is not obvious, however, why constraints on negative liberty should be viewed as more important and significant autonomy violations than constraints on positive autonomy. Why are some choice sets considered too constrained to permit autonomous choice making while other choice sets that are also constrained in some way are thought to retain enough options as to not make autonomous decision making impossible?

51. Of course, some choices women make are coerced in the traditional sense. Feminist claims that women are forced to commodify their sexuality because of threats of violence against them easily fit under the rubric of coercion. Feminists can uncontroversially argue that women who are kidnapped, physically threatened, and beaten in order to get them to sell their sexuality are not making valid choices worthy of our respect and enforcement. The choices are socially recognized as unfree and subject to challenge and invalidation.

52. In this case we have simply come to define the seductive offer itself as a rights violation.

53. Margaret Jane Radin, "Market-Inalienability," *Harvard Law Review* 100 (1987): 1906.

54. Radin, "Market-Inalienability," p. 1906; Margaret Jane Radin, "What, If Anything, Is Wrong with Baby Selling?" *Pacific Law Journal* 26 (1995): 145.

55. Radin, "What, If Anything, Is Wrong with Baby Selling?" p. 145.

56. Most people would also argue that the professor's proposal is inappropriate because grades should not be exchanged for personal services unrelated to a particular course's academic mission. In addition, grades should not be conditioned on certain activities for some students and different activities for other students. However, I am arguing that we find these proposals problematic not just because of how the professor is violating his ethical obligations to grade students based on the merit of their work, but also because of what the proposal does to the student who is forced to choose. The proposal is both coercive *and* unethical.

57. Dworkin's own view of autonomy focusing on the congruence of first- and second-order preferences faces the same problems of subjectivity. People will probably differ in whether they want to form their first-order desires under conditions in which they are presented with certain seductive-offer choice sets. The problem of subjectivity is avoided in Dworkin's consideration of threats because he simply assumes that individuals prefer not to form their preferences under conditions involving clear threats to their rights.

5. Socialization Critiques

1. See Priscilla Alexander, "Prostitution: A Difficult Issue for Feminists," in Frédérique Delacoste and Priscilla Alexander, eds., *Sex Work: Writings by Women in the Sex Industry* (Pittsburgh: Cleis Press, 1987); Catharine MacKinnon, "Prostitution and Civil Rights," *Michigan Journal of Gender & Law* 1

(1993): 13; Dorchen Leidholdt, "Prostitution: A Violation of Women's Human Rights," *Cardozo Women's Law Journal* 1 (1993): 133; Susan Kay Hunter, "Prostitution Is Cruelty and Abuse to Women and Children," *Michigan Journal of Gender & Law* 1 (1993): 91.

2.   Catharine MacKinnon, *Toward a Feminist Theory of the State* (Cambridge: Harvard University Press, 1989), p. 147.

3.   See generally, MacKinnon, *Toward a Feminist Theory of the State*; MacKinnon, "Prostitution and Civil Rights"; Catharine MacKinnon, "Feminism, Marxism, Method, and the State: Toward a Feminist Jurisprudence," *Signs* 8, no. 4 (1983): 636.

4.   Robin West, "The Difference in Women's Hedonic Lives: A Phenomenological Critique of Feminist Legal Theory," *Wisconsin Women's Law Journal* 3 (1987): 94.

5.   West, "The Difference in Women's Hedonic Lives," p. 92.

6.   West, "The Difference in Women's Hedonic Lives," p. 93.

7.   West, "The Difference in Women's Hedonic Lives," p. 93.

8.   As I will argue later in this chapter, I think feminists' real concern is about the choices themselves rather than the method of socialization by which one comes to desire them. That is, it is bad to think of oneself as a sex pet regardless of the reasons.

9.   Once an individual has been socialized to hold a certain set of preferences, even if this socialization took place through threats, she is no longer acting in accordance with someone else's will, as she was in the case of choices directly coerced by threatened rights violations, but is instead acting upon her own will.

10.   To some extent, I am proving a negative. As the examples in this chapter and those in chapter 2 illustrate, feminists have devoted significant energy to criticizing women's choices to sexually objectify or commodify themselves. Feminists have not devoted any time to criticizing women's choices to become doctors, lawyers, or professors. I assume from their silence that feminists are critical of the first set of choices but not of the second.

11.   Kathryn Abrams, "Sex Wars Redux: Agency and Coercion in Feminist Legal Theory," *Columbia Law Review* 95 (1995): 348.

12.   Abrams, "Sex Wars Redux," p. 348.

13.   See generally Kathryn Abrams, "Ideology and Women's Choices," *Georgia Law Review* 24 (1990): 761.

14.   Some research has, however, suggested a correlation between female promiscuity and an increased risk of rape. See David P. Bryden and Roger C. Park, "'Other Crimes' Evidence in Sex Offense Cases," *Minnesota Law Review* 78 (1994): 529 (explaining that "[s]tatistically, women who have had numerous sexual partners are more likely to live in high crime areas, or to engage in high-risk behavior, or both").

15.   These particular arguments were discussed in the previous section.

16.   See MacKinnon, *Toward a Feminist Theory of the State*, pp. 110–11: "Gender

socialization is the process through which women come to identify themselves as . . . sexual beings, as beings that exist for men, specifically for male sexual use. It is that process through which women internalize (make their own) a male image of their sexuality as their identity as women, and thus make it real in the world."

17. See West, "The Difference in Women's Hedonic Lives," p. 127 (the feminist method of consciousness raising is the ideal process for discovering women's authentic desires).

18. See Rita Freedman, *Beauty Bound: Why We Pursue the Myth in the Mirror* (Lexington, Mass.: Lexington Books, 1986).

19. See Reva Landau, "On Making 'Choices,'" *Feminist Issues* (1992); Susan Okin, *Justice, Gender, and the Family* (New York: Basic Books, 1989), pp. 142–44. See also Joan C. Williams, "Deconstructing Gender," *Michigan Law Review* 87 (1989): 797.

20. One might argue that an egalitarian socialization can be neutral if it does not encourage individuals equally toward all pursuits but rather is equally indifferent to the choices people make. Such an attempt to discover a "neutral" socialization context in the form of indifference does not seem to have much real-world weight. It is hard to imagine what indifference in socialization would look like since all societies attach values and meanings to different positions. It is not clear that egalitarianism as equality of indifference would really differ from egalitarianism as equality of choice, and both, it seems, remain premised on the belief that women and men should be socialized in the same ways and toward the same activities.

21. The notion of equal socializing environments is subjective at any particular point in time but is also most likely dynamic across time. What equality means and what social changes it requires probably vary at different times in history.

22. The next chapter looks more systematically at the difficulty of defining what it means to treat women and men equally.

23. One might argue that there does exist a logical stopping point indicative of procedural purity when the individual reaches some equilibrium or resting point in her answers; that is, when the individual's responses have remained stable over a period of time. While I believe that it may be possible to reach a stable resting point after repeated questioning about one's feelings and opinions given a single and consistent line of questioning, I doubt that the end point of stability will be the same regardless of who the questioner is and how the consciousness-raising questioning is done. Neither the questioning process nor its logical stopping point can be neutrally determined.

6. Equality Arguments

1. Choice sets are simply the array of options one is presented with.

2. Catharine A. MacKinnon, "Prostitution and Civil Rights," *Michigan Journal of Gender & Law* 1 (1993): 28.

3.   Susan Kay Hunter, "Prostitution Is Cruelty and Abuse to Women and Children," *Michigan Journal of Gender & Law* 1 (1993): 96. In criticizing women's choices to sexually objectify themselves, Rita Freedman makes a similar argument about women's lack of other options. According to Freedman, "While many idols are denied to females, that of beauty object is subtly as well as overtly encouraged." Rita Freedman, *Beauty Bound: Why We Pursue the Myth in the Mirror* (Lexington, Mass.: Lexington Books, 1986), p. 37.

4.   Susan Okin, *Justice, Gender, and the Family* (New York: Basic Books, 1989), p. 142.

5.   Joan C. Williams, "Deconstructive Gender," *Michigan Law Review* 87 (1989): 831.

6.   It is also the case that the "number" of elements in a set is manipulable. Consider the choice set "clean house, practice law," which ostensibly has just two elements. The first element, though, could be broken down into separate elements (mopping, cleaning dishes, doing laundry, etc.), as could the second element (litigation, divorce counsel, tax planning).

7.   The Amishness choice probably looks different in these two choice sets not only because the substantive meaning of the Amish choice changes but also because one is less likely to want to be Amish when given a range of other options than when Amishness is the only choice. This change in the probability that one would choose Amishness in the two sets suggests a different reason for choice-set incommensurability that I discuss later in this section.

8.   *Wisconsin v. Yoder*, 406 U.S. 205 (1971).

9.   *Wisconsin v. Yoder*, pp. 208–209.

10. The fear seemed to be not only that more children would leave the Amish community but also that even those who chose to stay would have a different relationship to Amishness than their parents thought appropriate.

11. Fundamentalist religious parents made a similar, but unsuccessful, argument about the socializing effect of cosmopolitanism in *Mozert v. Hawkins County*, 827 F.2d 1058 (6th Cir. 1987). *Mozert* involved a challenge brought by fundamentalist Christian parents who objected to the reading series used by elementary students in Hawkins County, Tennessee. Like the parents in *Wisconsin v. Yoder*, the parents in *Mozert* believed that the mere exposure of their children to a whole range of ideas that did not accord with their fundamentalist views weakened the ability of their children to truly be fundamentalists. That is, the exposure to different and conflicting attitudes and ways of life took away the children's ability to be fundamentalist Christians in the way that their parents wanted them to be.

12. See Myra Sadker and David Sadker, *Failing at Fairness: How America's Schools Cheat Girls* (New York: Charles Scribner's Sons, 1994); Kristin S. Caplice, "The Case for Public Single-Sex Education," *Harvard Journal of Law and Public Policy* 18 (Fall 1994): 256; Susan Estrich, "Is There a Case for Single-Sex Education," *Seattle Post-Intelligencer*, Sunday, July 17, 1994.

13. See, e.g., Note, "Cheering on Women and Girls in Sports: Using Title IX to Fight Gender Role Oppression," *Harvard Law Review* 110 (1997): 1627; Wendy Olson, "Beyond Title IX: Toward an Agenda for Women and Sports in the 1990's," *Yale Journal of Law and Feminism* 3 (1990): 105; Denise K. Stellmach, "Title IX: Mandate for Equality in Collegiate Athletics," *Wayne Law Review* 41 (1994): 203.

14. See Syda Kosofsky, "Toward Gender Equality in Professional Sports," *Hastings Women's Law Journal* 4 (1993): 209.

15. See Frank Litsky, "Behind These Great Women Are Men: Male Students Help UConn's No. 1 Basketball Team Get Better," *New York Times*, Feb. 20, 1997, p. B-13 (describing scrimmages between the University of Connecticut women's varsity basketball team and male students).

16. This argument that the differences in women's and men's choices are a function of the social devaluation of women may hold more weight in contexts where sex is not relevant to the nature and quality of the activity involved. For example, it may seem more plausible to attribute the vast discrepancy between the amounts that male and female movie stars are paid to differences in the social valuation of women and men and of female and male movie characters because it is difficult to say that the quality or nature of men's acting is significantly different from that of women.

17. Achieving equal choices in cases where sex is a relevant distinction requires a significant incursion into liberal rights. To the extent that the greater opportunities available for male basketball players than for their female counterparts are caused by a genuine (non-status-based) preference for men's basketball over women's, achieving equality of choice sets requires overriding individuals' private and legitimate preferences. It is a strange and illiberal argument to claim that Lobo is entitled to have the same financial reward, fan adoration, and public acclaim as does Hill even though she is not valued as highly as he is by the market which would grant her such things.

18. See generally MacKinnon, "Prostitution and Civil Rights"; and Hunter, "Prostitution Is Cruelty and Abuse to Women and Children."

19. Okin, *Justice, Gender, and the Family*, p. 171.

7. Vulnerability-Based Choice Critiques

1. Catharine A. MacKinnon, "Prostitution and Civil Rights," *Michigan Journal of Gender & Law* 1 (1993): 25.

2. Nancy Erbe, "Prostitutes: Victims of Men's Exploitation and Abuse," *Journal of Law and Inequality* 2 (1984): 611–612.

3. Rita Freedman, *Beauty Bound: Why We Pursue the Myth in the Mirror* (Lexington, Mass.: Lexington Books, 1986), pp. 32–35.

4. Although the requirement that individuals possess self-respect is a weakly perfectionist claim, I accept Rawls's assertion that recognizing self-respect as

a primary good that all individuals need and desire does not itself put forth an interesting or substantial perfectionist principle. See John Rawls, *A Theory of Justice* (Cambridge: Harvard University Press, 1971).

5. Freedman, *Beauty Bound,* p. 37.

6. Margaret A. Baldwin, "Public Women and the Feminist State," *Harvard Women's Law Journal* 20 (1997): 83.

7. Susan Moller Okin, *Justice, Gender, and the Family* (New York: Basic Books, 1989), p. 152.

8. See, e.g., Harry M. Clor, *Public Morality and Liberal Society: Essays on Decency, Law, and Pornography* (Notre Dame, Ind.: University of Notre Dame Press, 1996), pp. 103–12 (comparing the limited liberal conception of harm with a more expansive conception of moral harm).

9. Okin, *Justice, Gender, and the Family,* pp. 151–52

10. Okin, *Justice, Gender, and the Family,* pp. 160–63.

11. In fact, it is not clear to what extent, if any, women suffer a decline in their standard of living immediately after divorce, or to what extent their decline is dependent upon their predivorce homemaking status. In the late 1980s Lenore Weitzman's often-quoted findings that "[j]ust one year after legal divorce, [m]en experience a 42 percent improvement in their postdivorce standard of living, while women experience a 73 percent decline" achieved the status of popular folklore. See Lenore J. Weitzman, *The Divorce Revolution: The Unexpected Social and Economic Consequences for Women and Children in America* (New York: Free Press, 1985). However, after other researchers were unable to replicate her findings using her data, Weitzman acknowledged in 1996 that her original figures had been incorrect. See Lenore J. Weitzman, "The Economic Consequences of Divorce Are Still Unequal: Comment on Peterson," *American Sociological Review* 61 (1996): 538 (stating that "[w]hile it is likely . . . that the gender gap is less than I reported, even if the post-divorce standards of living, as Peterson contends, drop an average of only about 30 percent for women, and rise only about 10 percent for men, that is still a 40 percent difference between the two—and that outcome is unconscionable for a legal system and a society committed to fairness, justice, and equality").

A more recent study which used after-tax rather than gross income figures and which took into account monetary transfers between the two households in addition to the payment of court-ordered spousal and child support awards concluded that men were only 2 percent better off and women 8 percent worse off after divorce. See Sanford L. Braver, "The Gender Gap in Standard of Living after Divorce: Vanishingly Small?" *Family Law Quarterly* 33 (1999): 130. Indeed, some scholars have questioned whether women are actually worse off at all after divorce. See Herbert Jacob, *Silent Revolution: The Transformation of Divorce Law in the United States* (Chicago: University of Chicago Press, 1988), p. 159.

These studies do not, however, show the extent to which women's drop in standard of living after divorce is affected by their predivorce employment status. That is, they do not show whether nonworking women indeed have a sharper drop in their standard of living after divorce than do working women. The recent studies do suggest, however, that overall, the drop in women's standard of living after divorce is not nearly as significant as previously believed.

12. Okin, *Justice, Gender, and the Family*, p. 151.

INTRODUCTION TO PART III

1. Despite the seeming oxymoron, I believe such a concept is meaningful.

2. See Richard Rorty, *Consequences of Pragmatism* (Minneapolis: University of Minnesota Press, 1982), p. 160; John Dewey, *Experience and Nature* (Chicago: Open Court Publishing Company, 1925), p. 31.

3. Margaret Jane Radin and Frank Michelman, "Pragmatist and Postructuralist Critical Legal Practice," *University of Pennsylvania Law Review* 139 (1991): 1046.

4. Dewey, *Experience and Nature*, p. 31.

5. For example, see Thomas C. Grey, "Holmes and Legal Pragmatism," *Stanford Law Review* 41 (1989): 798.

6. William James, *Pragmatism* (New York: Prometheus Books, 1991), p. 88.

7. As discussed previously, Nussbaum's perfectionism suffers not from abstraction but from a too narrow focus on ensuring primary goods.

8. James, *Pragmatism*, p. 101.

8. Four Perfectionist Principles

1. Margaret Jane Radin, "Market-Inalienability," *Harvard Law Review* 100 (1987): 1885–86.

2. Radin, "Market-Inalienability," pp. 1905–1906.

3. As will become more clear later in this discussion, I am not restricting my definition of friendship to any idealized selfless version. To the contrary, I include a range of kinds of friendships, even those based on mutual self-interest. What is important is not the purity or selflessness of feeling from one person to the other but the fact that it is a feeling and a desire for connection with that other person that motivates the relationship between the two.

4. Of course, friendships do sometimes emerge between people who also have a market relationship with each other, such as a disabled person and a caregiver; however, these friendships arise in spite of the commodified care relationship. A friendship might grow out of the caregiving relationship between a disabled person and her helper. But, I argue, the disabled person did not, and could not, hire the caregiver to be her "friend."

5. Aristotle, *The Nicomachean Ethics*, trans. David Ross (Oxford: Oxford University Press, 1991), pp. 195–97.

6.   Margaret Jane Radin, *Contested Commodities* (Cambridge: Harvard University Press, 1996), pp. 105–06.

7.   Radin, *Contested Commodities*, p. 108.

8.   Margaret Jane Radin, *Reinterpreting Property* (Chicago: University of Chicago Press, 1993), p. 84.

9.   Radin, *Contested Commodities*, p. 108. Of course, the market aspect of homes are reinforced by foreclosure and tenant eviction laws.

10.   Radin, *Contested Commodities*, p. 133.

11.   The colonization of a woman's body during intercourse is of course paradigmatic of the loss of physical control in prostitution. My emphasis here, however, is on the harm of selling control over one's body generally, not on the specific harm of penetration.

12.   I think that pornography would be much less problematic for feminists if the performers acted out their roles but the video was never shown, or there was no film in the camera. That is, if people performed in the pornography for money but no one else ever saw the pornography. What makes pornography troubling seems less about the fact that someone acted in it and more about the fact that so many of us learn what our sexuality is and means through pornography.

13.   Iris Marion Young, *Throwing Like a Girl and Other Essays in Feminist Philosophy and Social Theory* (Bloomington: Indiana University Press, 1990), p. 116.

14.   Young, *Throwing Like a Girl*, p. 116.

15.   Self-employment that involves little client or outside contact may not reap the same benefits. However, most independent workers must have a great deal of contact with other public-sphere organizations in order to maintain their business contacts.

16.   Immanuel Kant, *Groundwork of the Metaphysics of Morals*, trans. H. J. Paton (New York: Harper & Row, 1956), p. 96.

17.   This is especially difficult since I do not believe that this self-love requirement rules out the possibility of altruistic behavior.

18.   It may be the most important because it may be required for one to be able to do the other three.

19.   There is an increasing discrepancy in our society, and many others, between self-sufficiency and self-reliance. I am focusing here on the former. Many people today are self-sufficient in the sense that they can pay to satisfy their needs; very few people, however, are self-reliant in the sense of actually being able to satisfy their needs through their own labor. It may in fact be the case that the more self-sufficient an individual becomes, the less self-reliant she becomes if she begins to hire others to do the basic life chores that she used to perform herself. My focus here is on ensuring that people have the sense of security and stability that comes with self-sufficiency rather than the sense of competency and accomplishment that comes with self-reliance.

20.   Mary Wollstonecraft, *Vindication of the Rights of Woman*, ed. Miriam Brody Kramnick (New York: Penguin Books, 1976), p. 283.

21. John Stuart Mill and Harriet Taylor Mill, *Essays on Sex Equality,* ed. Alice S. Rossi (Chicago: University of Chicago Press, 1970), p. 74.

22. Mill and Taylor Mill, *Essays on Sex Equality,* p. 74.

23. Mill and Taylor Mill, *Essays on Sex Equality,* p. 105

24. John Stuart Mill, *The Subjection of Women,* ed. Sue Mansfield (Wheeling, Ill.: Harlan Davidson, 1980), p. 48. As will become clear later, the fourth perfectionist principle calls for more than Mill's assurance of formal access to occupations and yet less than Taylor's insistence on women's actual economic independence. It calls for women to have at all times real possibilities for their own self-support.

25. Virginia Woolf, *A Room of One's Own* (New York: Harcourt, Brace, and Company, 1929), p. 182.

26. Virginia Woolf, *Three Guineas* (New York: Harcourt Brace Jovanovich, 1966), p. 110.

27. Woolf, *Three Guineas,* p. 110.

28. David D. Gilmore, *Manhood in the Making: Cultural Concepts of Masculinity* (New Haven, Conn.: Yale University Press, 1990), p. 110.

29. See John Locke, *Two Treatises of Government,* ed. C. B. Macpherson (Indianapolis, Ind.: Hackett Publishing Company, 1980); Jean-Jacques Rousseau, *The Social Contract and the Discourses,* trans. G. D. H. Cole (London: Everyman's Library, 1973).

30. For a discussion of the importance of bargaining power within intimate relationships, see Rhona Mahony, *Kidding Ourselves: Breadwinning, Babies, and Bargaining Power* (New York: Basic Books, 1995).

31. Martha Chen, "A Matter of Survival: Women's Right to Employment in India and Bangladesh," in *Women, Culture, and Development: A Study of Human Capabilities,* ed. Martha Nussbaum and Jonathan Glover (Oxford: Clarendon Press, 1995), pp. 37–57.

32. The question of how this principle affects the severely handicapped who cannot work to support themselves is interesting and complex. I do think that dependence on others and an inability to care for oneself is part of what makes severe disability scary. The fourth principle does not, however, require self-reliance, which is probably impossible for the severely handicapped, but only self-sufficiency, which is probably not. The principle requires only that individuals have their own means to support themselves such that they are not financially dependent upon another individual. Those who are severely handicapped are in fact likely to have their own source of income from the government in the form of disability payments. Hence, although severe handicap may seem to impair human flourishing in certain ways related to one's dependence on others, it does not seem to constitute a bar to satisfaction of this particular principle's focus on self-sufficiency.

33. Of course, the very fact that one is receiving wages for housework transforms the work from private to public to a large degree. Since all individuals are de-

pendent to some degree on the financial well-being of the state, it seems that economic dependence on the state does not involve the same dangers of whimsical deprivation that dependence on particular other individuals entails.

9. Conclusion

1.   See Susan Okin, *Justice, Gender, and the Family* (New York: Basic Books, 1989), chapter 8.

Index

abortion, 153n34
Abrams, Kathryn, 81
agenda. *See* hidden agenda of feminists
Alexander, Priscilla, 12–13
Anderson, Elizabeth, 142–143n36
anti-sex-work feminists, 14–18
arguments, perfectionist, 5. *See also* feminists' arguments
Aristotle, on friendship, 113–114
autonomy: criticism of choices and, 140n2; and justifications of coercion, 63–64, 73–74, 153–155nn41–42,50,57; liberalism and, 5, 130, 139n19; perfectionist arguments and, 5; Raz and, 28–29

Baldwin, Margaret A., 15, 105–106, 145n66
Bangladesh, 127–128
Barry, Brian, 63
Bell, Laurie, 140n6
Burke, Edmund, 60–61, 153n32

Canadian Organization for the Rights of Prostitutes (CORP), 14, 140–141n14
career: choices men make, 2–4, 138nn10,12,17; choices women make, 2–4, 138nn10,12,17; and self-sufficiency principle, 123–128, 132, 162–164nn18–19,24,30,32–33
Chen, Martha, 43, 127–128
choice sets: context influences choices, 90–101; cosmopolitanism and, 90–91, 94; defined, 157n1; equality arguments and, 88–102, 157–159nn1,3,16–17; for men, 89, 97–101, 129, 131; inequality of, critiques and, 49; vulnerability-based critiques and, 107–108; for women, 88–102, 129, 131, 158–159nn3,16–17
choices men make: career, 2–4, 138nn10,12,17; choice sets for, 89, 97–101, 129, 131; context of, 4, 137n5; educational investment and, 3–4, 137n5, 149–150n89
choices women make: acceptable range of, 5; authentic choices, 83–87, 157nn20–23;

basis of choice, 132; career and, 2–4, 138nn10,12,17; coercion and, 13; coercion-based critiques of, 51–75, 150–151nn1–7; context of, 4, 137n5; cosmopolitanism and, 90–91, 94; criticism of (*see* criticism of certain choices women make); educational investment and, 3–4, 137n5, 149–150n89; equality arguments and, 88–102, 157–159nn1,3,16–17; feminist dialogue on, 134–136; how to live a good life and, 131–136; Hurka and, 31–34, 146n33; intellectual, moral development principle and, 119–121, 162n15; Nussbaum and, 41–46, 148–149nn71–72,78; paid employment and, 3, 121, 137–138nn2,10, 162n15; perfectionist principles and, 111–128; pluralistic perfectionism and, 5; pragmatic perfectionism and, 109–110; problematic choices, 11–26; Raz and, 28–31, 145–146nn7,16,21; seductive offers and, 64–74, 155nn51,56; seemingly bad choices, 7; selective-choice critiques and, 82–83; self-love principle and, 121–123, 162n17; sex-kitten options, 91–92, 96–97, 133; sexual noncommodification principle and, 111–119, 162nn11–12; Sher and, 34–40, 147–148nn50,64, 148n67; socialization critiques of, 76–87, 155–157nn1,8–10,14,20–23; unchallengeable in liberal terms, 130; vulnerability-based critiques and, 103–110, 159–161n4,11. *See also* commodification of sexuality; conditions for making choices; criticism of certain choices women make; homemaker, full-time; objectification of sexuality; perfectionism
coercion: autonomy-based justifications of, 63–64, 73–74, 153–155nn41–42,50,57; as basis of choice, 132; coercive political theories, fear of, 6; conventionalist justifications of, 60–62, 72, 153nn32,34–35; criticism of choices, 49, 51–75; equality arguments and, 88–102, 157–159nn1,3,6–17; Kantian justifications of, 59–60, 71–72; liberalism and, 130–131; neutral justifications of, 57–63; seductive-offers ver-

self-sufficiency principle and, 123–128, 132, 162–164nn18–19,24,30,32–33
equality arguments, 88–102, 157–159nn1,3,16–17
Erbe, Nancy, 18, 104, 142–143n36
exotic dancers, 6. *See also* sex work; sex worker

fashion modeling, 119, 132
Feinburg, Joel, 63
feminist totalitarian regime, unreal danger of, 134–136
feminists: anti-sex-work feminists, 14–18; hidden agenda of, 1, 128–129, 132; perfectionism and, 136; political sphere and, 133–136; selectivity of vulnerability-based choice critiques, 106–108; totalitarianism and, 6, 134–136
feminists' arguments: equality arguments and, 88–102, 157–159nn1,3,16–17; perfectionism and, 5, 49, 128, 132; on seductive-offers version of coercion, 70–71
Filer, Randall, 4
Freedman, Rita, 21, 84, 105, 144n48, 158n3
Fried, Charles, 61–62, 153n35
friendship, 113–114, 161nn3–4
Fuchs, Victor, 3, 137–138nn2,10
full-time homemaker. *See* homemaker, full-time
future vulnerability. *See* vulnerability, future

Galston, William, 5
gaze objects, 122–123
gender inequalities, 1–4, 88–102, 157–159nn1,3,16–17
Gerson, Kathleen, 22
Gilmore, David, 125
good life: beliefs concerning, 110, 136; how to live, 131–136; human flourishing seen as, 9; liberalism and, 135–136; perfectionism and, 27, 111–128
government, role of: abortion and, 153n34; coercion and, 60–62, 153n34; education and, 6, 133–136; Kantian rationales and, 60; Nussbaum and, 41–43, 149–150nn87–88; self-sufficiency and, 125; totalitarianism and, 6, 134–136

Haksar, Vinit, 27
hidden agenda of feminists, 1, 128–129, 132
homemaker, full-time: authentic choices and, 89; basis of choice, 132; criticism of choice, 11, 21–25, 51–83, 132, 150–151nn1–7, 156nn8–10,14; economic vulnerability of,

106–107, 160–161n11; liberal terms and, 130; Nussbaum and, 44; as problematic choice, 11; seductive offers and, 64–74, 155n51; self-love principle and, 122–123, 132; self-sufficiency principle and, 126–128, 163–164nn30,32–33; vulnerability-based choices and, 103–110, 159–161nn4,11
human flourishing: how to live, 131–136; Hurka and, 31–34, 37–40, 146n33; intellectual, moral development principle and, 119–121, 162n15; liberalism and, 130, 135–136; Nussbaum and, 46; perfectionism and, 9, 27, 49, 111–128; pornography and, 118–119, 162n12; prostitution and, 116–117, 162n11; Raz and, 29–30, 37–40; self-love principle and, 121–123, 162n17; self-respect and, 105–106; Sher and, 34–40, 147–148nn50,64,67; vulnerability-based choice critiques and, 103–110, 159–161nn4,11; what constitutes, 6, 9. *See also* perfectionism
Hunter, Susan Kay, 15, 88–89, 100–101, 158n3
Hurka, Thomas, 27–28, 31–34, 145–146nn2,33, 154n42

India, 127–128
intellectual and moral development principle, 119–121, 132, 162n15

James, William, 110
Johnson, Mary, 12
judgments. *See* criticism of certain choices women make; perfectionism; value-laden judgments

Kant, Immanuel, 59–60, 122

Landau, Reva, 22, 25, 84, 145n66
lap dancing, 117
Lehrman, Karen, 19, 21–22
liberalism: changing away from, 135–136; coercion and, 154n42; defined, 4; inadequacy of, 7; perfectionism and, 10; public-sphere participation and, 129–130; values and, 5, 139n20
Locke, John, 125–126

MacKinnon, Catharine, 14–18, 20, 77, 88, 100–101, 104, 118
meaningful life. *See* human flourishing
men. *See* choices men make
Mill, Harriet Taylor, 124
Mill, John Stuart, 30–31, 57, 124–125, 163n24

Miller, Peggy, 14
Morgan, Peggy, 13–14, 140–141n14

National Task Force on Prostitution, 12
Nozick, Robert C., 53, 55, 63–64
Nussbaum, Martha C.: on functional capabilities, 41–42, 148–149n72; on perfectionism, 41–46, 145n2, 148–149nn71–72,78; on prostitution, 140n12

objectification of sexuality: basis of choice, 132; criticism of choice, 18–21, 51–75, 132, 150–151nn1–7; defined, 4; fashion modeling and, 119, 132; liberalism and, 130; methods of, 19; pornography and, 20, 143–144n43; as problematic choice, 11; seductive offers and, 64–74, 155n51; self-love principle and, 122–123, 132; visual thingification and, 20; vulnerability-based choice critiques and, 103–110, 159–161nn4,11; women as decorative chairs, 119. See also criticism of certain choices women make; sex kitten
objections. See criticism of certain choices women make
Okin, Susan, 22–24, 84, 89, 100–101, 105–107, 134, 145n66

Pateman, Carol, 142–143n36
perfectionism: and acceptable choices, 5; anti-sex-work argument, 142–143n36; and choices women make, 5–6, 26, 103–110, 159–161nn4,11; coercive political theories and, 6; contemporary, 7; context-specific, 40; defined, 1, 9, 27; endorsement of, 6–7; equality arguments and, 88–102, 157–159nn1,3,16–17; feminists' arguments and, 49, 128, 132; four principles and, 111–128, 161–164nn3–4,11–12,15,17–19,24,32–33; frightens people, 5–6; gender inequalities and, 1; grounding of, 7, 40; Haksar on, 27; historical problems with, 111; as human flourishing, 1, 5 (see also human flourishing); Hurka, on, 27; liberalism and, 10, 135–136; moral theories and, 6, 111–128; open debate of, 132–136; pluralistic, 5; and policy and individual thinking, 134–136; political risks of, 6, 134–136; pragmatic, 7, 109–110; principles of (see perfectionist principles); private realm of behavior and, 6; pro-sex-work, 140–141n14; selectivity of vulnerability-based choice critiques; strong, 27; a theory is, when, 5 (see also perfectionist

theories); totalitarianism and, 6, 134–136; versions of, 129; weak, 27. See also human flourishing
perfectionist moral theories, 6; four perfectionist principles and, 111–128
perfectionist principles: to assess choices women make, 2; feminists and, 7; four perfectionist principles and, 111–128, 161–164nn3–4,11–12,15,17–19,24,32–33; friendship and, 113–114, 161nn3–4; intellectual and moral development principle, 119–121, 162n15; personal beliefs and, 113–114; self-love principle, 121–123, 162n17; self-sufficiency principle, 123–128, 162–164nn18–19,24,30,32–33; sexual noncommodification principle, 111–119, 162nn11–12; Yuracko and, 111–128, 162–164nn18–19,24,30,32–33
perfectionist theories: for criticism of choices women make, 9, 27; Hurka and, 31–34, 146n33; moral theories, 6; Nussbaum and, 41–46, 148–149nn71–72,78; Raz and, 28–31, 145–146nn7,16,21; Sher and, 34–40, 147–148nn50,64,67
Pheterson, Gail, 12
politics: advocacy of political change, 133; inclusion of feminist values in the political sphere, 133–136; political risks of perfectionism, 6; public-sphere participation and, 120, 129–130; Sher and, 34–40, 147–148nn50,64,67; totalitarianism and, 6, 134–136. See also government, role of
pornographic models, 6. See also sex work
pornography: effect on women, 20, 143–144n43; fashion modeling and, 119; Nussbaum and, 45; pornographic models and, 6; and sex kitten decision, 21; sexual noncommodification principle and, 118–119, 162n12
Posner, Richard, 57–58, 152nn19,22
pro-sex-work perfectionism, 140–141n14
prostitution: authentic choices and, 88–89, 158n3; as basis of choice, 132; and colonization of a woman's, 116, 162n11; criticism of choice, 12–15, 104, 131–132, 140–141n14; Nussbaum and, 45; sexual noncommodification principle and, 112–113, 116–117, 132, 162nn11–12
public-sphere participation, 119–121, 129–130, 132, 162n15

Radin, Margaret Jane, 110, 112, 114–115
rationality: Hurka and, 32–33; perfectionist

principles and, 120; Sher and, 34–40, 147–148nn50,64,67

Raz, Joseph, 28–31, 145–146nn2,7,16,21

rights-violation, threat of: choice critiques and, 76–83, 156nn8–10,14; coercion and, 52–55, 62–63; Dworkin (Gerald) and, 63, 154–155n50; Fried and, 62

Rosta, Eva, 13–14

Rousseau, Jean-Jacques, 125–126

Satz, Debra, 142n31

Scott, Valerie, 140–141n14

seductive offers: as coercion, 64–74, 155nn51,56–57; criticism of, 70–71; defined, 66; examples of, 67–70, 155n56; a good life and, 131; nonperfectionist rationales and, 71–74, 155n57

self-love principle, 121–123, 132, 162n17

self-objectification. See objectification of sexuality

self-respect: grounded in one's worth, 5; liberalism and, 5; perfectionism and, 5; self-love principle and, 121–123, 162n17; vulnerability-based choices and, 103–110, 159–161nn4,11

self-subsistence, 123–128, 162–164nn18–19,24,30,32–33

self-sufficiency principle, 123–128, 132, 162–164nn18–19,24,30,32–33

sex kitten: criticism of choice of, 11, 18–21, 51–83, 143–144nn40,48, 150–151nn1–5, 156nn8–10,14; defined, 139–140n1; Nussbaum and, 44; sex-kitten options and, 91–92, 96–97, 133

sex work: anti-sex-work feminists on, 14–18; criticism of choice of, 12–18, 140–141n14; Nussbaum and, 44; pro-sex-work perfectionism and, 140–141n14; seductive-offers coercion and, 64–74, 155n51. See also commodification of sexuality; pornography; prostitution; sex worker

sex worker: criticism of choice of, 11–18, 51–83, 103–110, 140–141n14, 150–151nn1–7, 156nn8–10,14, 159–161nn4,11; defined, 139–140n1; lap dancing and, 117, 162nn11–12; method of socialization-based choice critiques and, 76–83; pornography and, 118–119, 132, 162n12; seductive offers and, 64–74, 155nn51,56–57; sexual noncommodification principle and, 111–119, 132, 162nn11–12. See also commodification of sexuality; pornography; prostitution; sex work

sexual noncommodification principle,
162nn11–12; prostitution and, 112–113, 116–117, 132, 162nn11–12

sexuality: effect of market in sexuality on, 115; fashion modeling and, 119; lap dancing and, 117; pornography and, 118–119, 162n12; real sexuality and, 111, 114; sexual noncommodification principle and, 111–119, 132, 162nn11–12. See also commodification of sexuality; objectification of sexuality

Sher, George, 28, 34–40, 147–148nn50,64,67, 154n42

single way of life, 5

socialization: and authentic choices, 83–87, 157nn20–23; criticism of certain choices women make, 49, 76–102, 155–157nn1,8–10,14,20–23, 157–159nn1,3,16–17; and sex kitten decision, 20–21; and sex worker decision, 16–18; social subsidies, social marginalization and, 6; and visual thingification, 20

status quo violation, 55–57, 62

Sunstein, Cass, 63

thingification, visual, 20

threatened-status-quo version of coercion, 55–57

totalitarianism, 6, 134–136

value-laden judgments, 4–5, 81–82, 131. See also criticism of certain choices women make

visual thingification, 20

vulnerability, future: criticism of certain choices women make, 49, 103–110, 159–161nn4,11; full-time homemaker and, 24–25, 103, 105–107, 145n66, 160–161n11; objectification of sexuality and, 105, 107; self-love principle and, 122–123; sex kitten and, 20–21; sex worker and, 18, 103–104

Waldron, Jeremy, 40

Weinrib, Ernest, 63

Wertheimer, Alan, 53, 55–56

West, Robin, 77–78

WHISPER (Women Hurt in Systems of Prostitution Engaged in Revolt), 15, 17–18

Williams, Joan, 22, 24–25, 89, 100–101

Wolf, Naomi, 19–20

Wollstonecraft, Mary, 123–124

Women Hurt in Systems of Prostitution Engaged in Revolt. See WHISPER

Woolf, Virginia, 125

Young, Iris Marion, 110

KIMBERLY A. YURACKO received her Ph.D. in Political Science from Stanford University and her J.D. from Stanford Law School. She has written several articles on feminist political theory, anti-discrimination law, and gender equity in college athletics. She is currently Assistant Professor of Law at Northwestern University School of Law.